Mapping Dialogue

Essential Tools for Social Change

Marianne Mille Bojer
Heiko Roehl
Marianne Knuth
Colleen Magner

Taos Institute Publications
Chagrin Falls, Ohio

Mapping Dialogue

Essential Tools for Social Change

FIRST EDITION
Cover photo by Heiko Roehl

ISBN-10: 0-9712312-8-1   PRINTED IN U.S.A. and the UK

ISBN-13: 978-0-9712312-8-3

LCN: 2008929497

Taos Institute Publications

The Taos Institute is a nonprofit organization dedicated to the development of social constructionist theory and practices for the purpose of world benefit. Constructionist theory and practice locates the source of meaning, value

and action in communicative relations among people. Chief importance is placed on relational process and its outcomes for the welfare of all. Taos Institute Publications offers contributions to cutting-edge theory and practice in social construction. These books are designed for scholars, practitioners, students and the openly curious. The Taos Institute's newest series is the **Taos Tempo Series: Collaborative Practices for Changing Times**. The **Focus Book Series** provides brief introductions and overviews that illuminate theories, concepts and useful practices. The **Books for Professionals Series** provides in-depth works, focusing on recent developments in theory and practice. Books in all three series are particularly relevant to social scientists and to practitioners concerned with individual, family, organizational, community and societal change.

Kenneth J. Gergen
President, Board of Directors
The Taos Institute

Taos Institute Board of Directors

Focus Book Series Editors
Harlene Anderson, Jane Seiling, Jackie Stavros

Books For Professionals Series Editor
Kenneth J. Gergen

General Taos Institute Publications Editor
Mary Gergen

Executive Director
Dawn Dole

For information about the Taos Institute and social constructionism visit:
www.taosinstitute.net

Taos Institute Publications

Focus Book Series

The Appreciative Organization, Revised Edition (2008) by Harlene Anderson, David Cooperrider, Ken Gergen, Mary Gergen, Sheila McNamee, Jane Watkins and Diana Whitney

Appreciative Inquiry: A Positive Approach to Building Cooperative Capacity, (2005) By Frank Barrett and Ronald Fry

Dynamic Relationships: Unleashing the Power of Apprecitive Inquiry in Daily Living, (2005) by Jacqueline Stavros and Cheri B. Torres

Appreciative Sharing of Knowledge: Leveraging Knowledge Management for Strategic Change, (2004) by Tojo Thatchekery

Social Construction: Entering the Dialogue, (2004) by Kenneth J. Gergen and Mary Gergen

Appreciative Leaders: In the Eye of the Beholder, (2001) Edited by Marge Schiller, Bea Mah Holland, and Deanna Riley

Experience AI: A Practitioner's Guide to Integrating Appreciative Inquiry and Experiential Learning, (2001) by Miriam Ricketts and Jim Willis

Books for Professionals Series

Conversational Realities Revisited: Life, Language, Body and World, (2008) by John Shotter

Horizons in Buddhist Psychology: Practice, Research and Theory, (2006) edited by Maurits Kwee, Kenneth J. Gergen and Fusako Koshikawa

Therapeutic Realities: Collaboration, Oppression and Relational Flow, (2005) by Kenneth J. Gergen

SocioDynamic Counselling: A Practical Guide to Meaning Making, (2004) by R. Vance Peavy

Experiential Exercises in Social Construction – A Fieldbook for Creating Change, (2004) by Robert Cottor, Alan Asher, Judith Levin, Cindy Weiser

Dialogues About a New Psychology, (2004) by Jan Smedslund

Taos Tempo Series: Collaborative Practices for Changing Times

Mapping Dialogue: Essential Tools for Social Change, (2008) by Marianne Mille Bojer, Heiko Roehl, Mariane Knuth-Hollesen, Colleen Magner

Positive Family Dynamics: Appreciative Inquiry Questions to Bring Out the Best in Families, (2008) by Dawn Cooperrider Dole, Jen Hetzel Silbert, Ad Jo Mann, Diana Whitney

For on-line ordering of books from Taos Institute Publications visit
www.taosinstitutepublications.net, Email: info@taosoinstitute.net

For further information, please call: 1-888-999-TAOS, 1-440-338-6733

To those whose voices need to be heard in dialogue

Table of Contents

Foreword

The complexity of global challenges today and our increasing inter-dependence demand of us all to seek solutions through engaging with others. The need for a culture of participation and democracy has never been greater. This is obvious when one scans the state of the world's democracy in addressing its citizens' problems. The many problems affecting society remain unaddressed, either because of failure for the parties involved in the conflict to come together or due to the undermining of democratic institutions and weakening of governance as a result.

Nelson Mandela's life is based on dialogue. It is through his work and those of others that the negotiated peaceful transition from apartheid to democracy was facilitated. South Africa's success in negotiated settlements remains as a beacon for the world. It was driven by the need to free its citizens from the shackles of apartheid and create a just society for all to live and realize their true potential.

> 'I have always endeavoured to listen to what each and every person in a discussion had to say before venturing my own opinion.'
>
> Nelson Mandela

The Nelson Mandela Foundation Centre of Memory and Dialogue aims to develop and sustain dialogue around Mr. Mandela's legacy. It is committed to utilizing the history, experience, values, vision and leadership of its Founder to provide a non-partisan platform for public discourse and contributes to the making of a just society by convening dialogue around critical social issues. Achieving participation in decision-making, even at policy levels, is prioritized.

We have convened multi-stakeholder dialogues to address various issues such as access to education, access to HIV/AIDS Antiretroviral Treatment in communities living in poorly resourced areas, the plight of children orphaned and made vulnerable by poverty and HIV/AIDS, gender inequality, human rights, and the role of the media in reporting critical social issues impacting on society among others.

This valuable resource book on dialogue methodologies comes at the right time when practitioners and others involved in finding solutions for intractable societal problems need broader understanding of the tools available to achieve sustainable social change. We are confident that the reader will derive as much benefit from this book as we have.

Dr Mothomang Diaho

Head of the Dialogue Programme
Centre of Memory and Dialogue
Nelson Mandela Foundation

Please visit: www.nelsonmandela.org

Introduction

Of course we were excited. When we met in summer 2005 to talk about supporting the Nelson Mandela Foundation's Dialogue work, we all felt that we were involved in a project of great significance. A project that promised to truly contribute and make a difference.

At that time, Mille, Marianne and Colleen were involved in a wide range of engagements as Dialogue Practitioners. Mille was in the midst of launching a multi-stakeholder "Change Lab" addressing the crisis of orphaned and vulnerable children in South Africa; Colleen was busy managing an extensive dialogue programme at one of South Africa's leading business schools, and Marianne was running an innovative rural learning village in Zimbabwe. Meanwhile, Heiko spent his last two years as a resident consultant at the Nelson Mandela Foundation in Johannesburg, South Africa. He was seconded by the German Government to support the Organizational Development of the Foundation through the German Technical Co-Operation (GTZ). In that year, the Board of Trustees of the Foundation had decided to focus a significant part of the Foundation's work on Dialogue, which is regarded as an indispensable part of the Founder's legacy. During and since South Africa's transition to democracy, Nelson Mandela had exhibited a formidable ability to forgive, along with an awareness of the importance of listening to all sides with a genuine recognition that everyone holds a piece of the puzzle of the future, and everyone needs to be involved in moving forward together.

Jointly with the Management Team of the Foundation, we endeavored to draw on our experience of different dialogue methodologies and approaches to create an overview on the various tools for dialogue, their specific attributes, advantages and shortfalls. We wanted to make sure that it would become a practical and usable resource - instead of an academic exercise - and so we looked for illustrative case studies, easy-to-use checklists and a section that would allow an overall assessment of the tools portrayed so the reader would be able to determine potential usefulness for a given situation.

Over and above this immediate mandate to explore ways in which dialogue can be used to address social challenges in South Africa by the Foundation, we were hoping that this material would be useful to

11

anyone who shares our interest and our desire to improve the quality of human conversations.

The outcome was a report entitled *Mapping Dialogue. A Research project profiling dialogue tools and processes for social change.* We decided to make the report available to a wider audience on the Pioneers of Change website which proved to be an excellent idea. The report received significant attention, and we got positive and encouraging comments and feedback from all over the world. Many communities involved in social development recommended the study and added the link to their sites.

We have, however, always been conscious about the fact that the internet does not reach everywhere. Also, we knew that we might miss out on practitioners who simply enjoy taking a handbook along when going into the field. As a result, the idea for this book was born in a small café in Melville, Johannesburg in winter 2006.

The modern world loves answers. We like to solve problems quickly. We like to have a clear picture of the way ahead. We like to know what to do. We don't want to "reinvent the wheel" and "waste our time". And when we have the answers or a wheel

> 'An answer is always the part of the road that is behind you. Only questions point to the future.'
>
> Jostein Gaarder

invented, we are keen on passing the information on to others: Through the media, through training programs where teachers pass on answers to students, or through conferences where experts speak on panels while hundreds listen (or pretend to listen) in the audience. This approach to human conversation may be useful for some situations, but for two reasons, it has become particularly problematic when working on the social challenges of the 21st century.

Firstly, we live in a world of increasing complexity and inter-relatedness, where answers have a short life-span. Not all problems are complex, but most if not all of the major social issues are. Poverty, HIV/AIDS and Crime are perfect examples.

Secondly, it seems that people have an inherent desire to solve their *own* problems. Human beings have a living, deep impetus for freedom and self-determination. We find that given the appropriate circumstances, people are usually more resourceful than expected in terms of finding their own solutions to the problem they face. When formulaic responses are imported or imposed from the outside, they meet resistance and often fail. This is partly because they are not exactly appropriate in the given context, but just as much because there is a lack of ownership from people who haven't participated or been consulted in the decision-making.

Even if only for these two reasons, as agents of change, we need to be adept at asking questions, and at talking and listening to each other. These are age-old competencies. For millennia, people in villages across the world have worked through collective challenges, creating solutions through conversation. But many of us seem to have forgotten how to engage in, and be present to, conversations. In these times of information overload, electronic communication, scientific rationality, and organizational complexity, it sometimes feels like we have forgotten how to talk to each other. The art of conversation appears to be on the decline.

The amount of time and resources globally invested in technological development over the past centuries is inconceivable. The results we observe today are equally incredible. Now, at the beginning of this century, we are able to take a look into the origins of the universe through space-based telescopes, discover what happens if the smallest of the smallest particles, protons, collide in particle physics laboratories and marvel at a myriad of other technological wonders created with tireless effort, over centuries and centuries. It seems ironic that, at the same time, we often still communicate and solve problems the same way we did hundreds of years ago. Or, as said above, worse. Looking at the world in 2008, it seems that the evolution of human conversation still has a long way to go.

Using this book

In navigating the field of conversation and dialogue, it became apparent to us that the term is very broad. In one of the interviews on which this book is based, it was pointed out that dialogue includes dialogue with oneself, dialogue with nature, dialogue with the past and future, and online dialogue. In order to keep the focus, we decided to narrow down to *dialogue methods applicable to face-to-face gatherings of groups of people meeting to address collective social challenges.*

The approaches (or tools) we selected within this focus are diverse in many ways. Some are designed for small groups of 20 people, while others can accommodate up to 1200 or even 5000 in dialogue at the same time. Some focus on exploring and resolving conflict and differences, while others emphasize looking first to what is working and agreed upon. Some are explicitly dialogues between groups while others require each participant to be there only as themselves, as individuals. However, looking across all of these dialogue methods, some clear, common patterns emerge.

All the tools focus on enabling open communication, honest speaking, and genuine listening. They allow people to take responsibility for their own learning and ideas. They create a safe space or "container" for people to surface their assumptions, to question their previous perceptions, judgments and worldviews, and to change the way they think. They generate new ideas or solutions that go beyond what anyone had thought of before. They create a different level of understanding of people and problems. They allow for more contextual and holistic ways of seeing.

The variety of dialogue methods available to us today have emerged in different situations but in response to quite similar needs and discoveries. They are part of a wider shift that is happening as complexity and diversity increase and people become more aware of their interdependence, and hence their need to hear each other, to understand, and to collaborate.

This collection profiles ten Dialogue methods in depth and a number of others more superficially. The book is organized in three parts:

- The first, *Foundations*, offers explanations on the generic foundations for a good dialogue process. These are aspects that are overarching; they represent the basis for the actual toolkit and should be read beforehand.

- The second part is the actual *Toolkit*. This is where you find the in-depth explanation of 10 methods as well as brief descriptions of additional tools. Each of the 10 methods contains a method fingerprint displaying the specific characteristics of the tool, a review of applications, a case example, and our subjective commentary. The methods have simply been ordered alphabetically.

- Finally, our *Epilogue* honors the African tradition of conversation, going to the deep roots and heritage of many of these processes.

Each of the profiled dialogue tools has a life story behind it. Many of these stories begin with someone posing a question.

- Given that the coffee breaks seem to be the most useful part of the conference anyway, what if the whole conference was designed similar to a coffee break?

- What is being lost when we just take majority decisions and don't hear what the minority has to say?

- How do the questions we ask shape our reality?

- How do we create a networked conversation, modeled on how people naturally communicate?

- Why are we re-creating the same conference rituals when they are passifying us and limiting our creativity?

- Why are we not managing to bring in the collective intelligence of hundreds of people but rather choosing over and over to just listen to a few expert voices?

A Dialogue Dictionary

The most common dictionary definition of a dialogue is simply *a conversation between two or more people*. In the field of dialogue practitioners, however, it is given a much deeper and more distinct meaning. David Bohm went back to the source of the word, deriving from the Greek root of "dia" which means "through" and "logos" which is "the word" or "meaning", and therefore saw dialogue as meaning flowing through us. Elements of this deeper understanding of the word include an emphasis on questions, inquiry, co-creation, and listening, the uncovering of one's own assumptions and those of others, a suspension of judgment and a collective search for truth. Bill Isaacs calls dialogue a conversation "with a center, not sides".

What is Dialogue Not?

Advocacy. Advocacy is the act of pleading or arguing strongly in favor of a certain cause, idea or policy.

Conference. A conference is a formal meeting for consultation or discussion.

Consultation. In a consultation, a party with the power to act consults another person or group for advice or input to a decision. The decision-maker generally retains the power to take the advice or not.

Debate. A debate is a discussion usually focused around two opposing sides, and held with the objective of one side winning. The winner is the one with the best articulations, ideas and arguments.

Discussion. As opposed to dialogue, Bohm points out that the root of the word discussion, "cuss", is the same as the root of "percussion" and "concussion", meaning to break apart. A discussion is generally a rational and analytical consideration of a topic in a group, breaking a topic down into its constituent parts in order to understand it.

Negotiation. A negotiation is a discussion intended to produce an agreement. Different sides bring their interests to the table, and the negotiation has a transactional and bargaining character to it.

Salon. A salon is a periodic social, unstructured, and informal gathering involving conversation with no particular objective.

Acknowledgements

We would like to acknowledge a number of people who have contributed to this research by supporting it, emailing us documents, sending us feedback, and/or taking time to talk to us face-to-face or over the phone.

They include: Verne Harris, Mothomang Diaho, Naomi Warren, Shaun Johnson, Elaine McKay, Zelda la Grange, John Samuel, Busi Dlamini, Doug Reeler, Nomvula Dlamini, Gavin Andersson, Ishmael Mkhabela, Njabulo Ndebele, Teddy Nemeroff, Bjorn Brunstad, Carsten Ohm, Tim Merry, Mogomme Alpheus Masoga, Myrna Lewis, Zaid Hassan, Nick Wilding, Bob Stilger, Kate Parrot, Bettye Pruitt, Leon Olsen, Anthony Blake and last but not least Ken and Mary Gergen, who encouraged us to publish this book in the Taos Institute Series.

Inviting your input

In the spirit of dialogue, we are interested in receiving feedback on this book and its usefulness to dialogue practitioners. We would like to continue collecting material on Dialogue Tools. Any reading material, books, or articles, feedback, reflections, and input to the content of this book from your experience will be greatly appreciated. We look forward to hearing from you on mappingdialogue@mail.com .

We have greatly enjoyed this process, and are left deeply impressed with all the work we have found going on in this field. We look forward to continuing the journey, and to experimenting with the new knowledge we have gained.

Sao Paulo/Frankfurt/Harare/Johannesburg

Marianne Mille Bojer

Heiko Roehl

Marianne Knuth

Colleen Magner

I. Foundations

The dialogue methods portrayed in this book appear as if they are separate, independent tools, each one with its own history, purpose and attributes. With this section, we intend to dispel this notion by presenting some of the underlying principles of successful dialogue processes. These principles provide a sense of how the tools are connected, and what is required to design integral processes of change and learning, be it for small groups of a few people, or gatherings and processes of several hundreds.

This section is meant to guide your reflection process as you work through your design, making choices about process, flow, and which of the many tools for dialogue and interaction are those most suitable for your specific situation.

Clarity of Purpose

Before deciding on which tools to make use of, we need to be crystal clear on our intention: Why are we bringing this group of people together? What purpose lies behind this specific process of change? What is this whole thing about? Sometimes we may find ourselves having begun something without quite knowing why, or for reasons that are inappropriate or outside of the particular context and the needs of the people involved. Within most, if not all of the tools we are presenting, lies the essential principle of the clarity of purpose.

Before clarifying a purpose, it can be necessary to connect with the need to which the process is responding. What are the specific needs that have brought us together? What do we hope to achieve as we respond to it? From a truthful, genuine need, clear purpose can

> 'Clarity of purpose is a sweet weapon against confusion'
>
> Toke Moeller

be derived. It's also important to be conscious on whether the investment of time and attention we are demanding from the participants is within reasonable balance with their perception of the process' ability to meet their needs.

The purpose needs to be attractive for all participants. It is very important not to formulate it in too specific, structured terms, such as quantifiable goals. Overly explicit objectives and specified expectations towards the outcome have the tendency to become quite dominant in the process, which can deter openness and dialogue. Some proponents and practitioners of dialogue emphasize that on the one hand, it needs to be completely open-ended and not attached to specific outcomes, on the other there needs to be clarity on why the group is coming together.

Good Questions

The power of a good question cannot be underestimated. Good questions are catalytic. They open up the learning field. They stimulate thought processes, curiosity, and the desire to engage with a group, and they are central to what defines and distinguishes dialogue.

Often we arrive to meetings with answers and expertise, statements to be discussed, or positions to be advocated or negotiated. But in dialogue, questions are in many ways more powerful than answers. Questions pull people towards the future, while answers refer to the past. A question that has meaning to the people involved can ignite the whole process of learning and change. It opens up the field and fosters engagement with meaningful issues. Bill Isaacs describes dialogue as a "conversation with a center, not sides", that "center" is often created by one or more good questions.

It is an art to identify powerful questions that provide meaning to a group of people, a community, or a nation. These are questions that can come alive inside of us, as we seek to work with them. The greatest questions come directly from the field (the hearts and minds) of the people involved. Good questions have the ability to give dialogues on complex issues a frame without containing them. For example, there might be one or more overriding question/s guiding an entire process. Or, an initial question can be questioned, refined and be used as a mirror for joint reflection. Questions are an integral part of most of the tools we present in this book.

Participation and participants

Our dialogue work originates from a belief in the intelligence and wisdom that is accessible to us in each person, with whom we connect and engage. Depending on the purpose, different forms and levels of participation are required to achieve a successful dialogue. Many dialogue methods support the work of going from fragmentation to wholeness through *inclusiveness*. As we find ways of connecting and including different voices and parts of a system, surprising and new discoveries can be made.

> **These questions can help clarifying dialogue participation and participants:**
>
> - Based on our purpose, who needs to be involved?
>
> - What do we hope to do and achieve with them?
>
> - What will each of them be bringing and what will they be wanting to gain?
>
> - Do we trust that they each hold an invaluable part of the puzzle we are trying to solve?
>
> - How do we best involve and engage them?

If time and resources allow, it can make a big difference to interview all or some of the participants in advance of a workshop. This has many benefits: It lays the foundation for planning, it indicates to the participants that their voice is appreciated, and it gets everyone involved in thinking about the topic in advance.

The ultimate level of inclusion is when the participants step into a role of co-hosts. In this role, the group's leadership and facilitation is completely shared. This is of course not possible with hundreds of participants. However, imagining what a maximum of involvement and engagement would look like can help us make the most of the participants' time and resources.

Underlying Process Structure

There is an underlying rhythm to most successful change processes. Some of the tools and processes we portray here have integrated their own understanding of deep-rooted change into their proposed workshop designs. For many of the tools though, we need to design an overall workshop flow of activities and a daily rhythm that supports our intentions. There are several models that can help us think through the most appropriate underlying structure of a process. One simple version is the model of divergence and convergence. The divergent phase of a process is a time of opening up possibilities, issues, or themes. It is about generating alternatives, gathering diverse points of view, allowing disagreement in and suspending judgment. We are often afraid of opening up to allow for real divergence to occur, because we are uncomfortable or even fearful of the messiness of too many new and divergent ideas and perspectives. Yet the greater the divergence, the freedom of voicing wild ideas, at the beginning of a process, the greater the possibility of surprising and innovative outcomes.

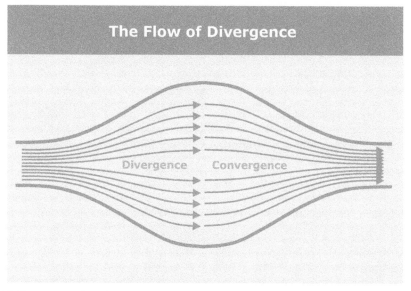

The Flow of Divergence

Divergence   Convergence

If divergence is all that occurs, however, we risk facing frustration and the process will not render positive results. Convergence is therefore as important to plan for and build into the process. It is about arriving at, and making explicit, the conclusions, insights, and next steps of the process, and perhaps what the newly developed, shared questions are. The two movements of divergence and convergence can take place multiple times during a process, and they can also occur as one pattern. Some tools are better suited for supporting divergence, others for convergence.

Transformative dialogue processes that truly allow for divergence often include a "groan zone" or "grey fog" situation in the middle. The groan zone is that somewhat painful place, where everything is a little too chaotic, unclear and unstructured. Sometimes this is a time of conflict and "storming"; sometimes it's characterized more by confusion and feeling overwhelmed by complexity or even despairing. This phase is an indispensable part of any process of certain depth. It is here that innovation and breakthrough have a real chance of occurring. When the group manages to stay with the messiness for a little while, and then enters into a process of convergence, they can experience major changes. On the other hand, if divergence is less, and convergence is premature, the potential is lower for major shifts to occur.

In their underlying architectures, different tools emphasize different process structures. Some of the tools have a distinct architecture and a flow associated with them. They have a storyline or a set of specified phases they move participants through. For example, the Change Lab process works with a very specific structure, in broad strokes following the general principle of allowing initial divergence followed by very clear convergence, with a phase of "emergence" in between. Future Search moves through looking at the past, then the present, and finally the future. Other methods like World Café or Circle are less focused on flow and can easily be incorporated as a tool into a variety of processes.

Principles

Principles define how we would like to be together as we pursue our purpose. Principles can be used to design and guide the process and the involvement of participants. Even if we just come together as an informal group for a conversation of a few hours, making a simple set of agreements for how we want to be together is important. The longer and larger an initiative the more critical working through principles together becomes. Most of the tools here have a set of principles attached to them, and this is a significant part of what makes them work. Some examples include: "Rotate leadership" (Circle), "Access the wisdom of the minority" (Deep Democracy), "Explore questions that matter" (World Café) and "Whoever comes are the right people" (Open Space).

Often a convener will share (or co-create) the purpose and principles with participants both before and at the beginning of an event or process, and where possible allow for its evolution during the process with the broader group of participants. The group, not just the convener, should "own" the purpose and principles. Taken as a whole, a clear purpose together with the principles provides a compass helping us to navigate and make decisions about how to move forward.

Tool Selection

All tools have a tendency to strongly guide and inform the behavior of those who use them. Tool-specific expertise can quickly lead into tool-related dependence. The tools we portray here have their own histories, philosophies and worldviews. They invite the user to identify with the tool and to share the way the tool looks at the world, defines problems and offers solutions. If we have gained enough expertise to use the tool, it makes us feel comfortable and safe. We are able to explain what is going on through the interpretations the tool is offering us. Many dialogue tools claim to have universal applicability across cultures, group sizes, and situations.

This process unfolds whenever tool-related expertise is developed, and it bears a great risk that is best expressed by the proverb: "With a hammer in your hand, the whole world looks like a nail". The ideal way to deal with this problem is to consciously select and use tools in a way that puts the purpose of the dialogue at hand first. In order to benefit from the potential a tool is offering it is very important to be aware of its limitations. Continuously discovering new methods and drawing on a broad repertoire in a "mix-and-match" type of approach helps.

The Facilitator

The tools, the design, the process: It is easy to let concerns around these issues preoccupy us, and yet the most important tool that we have at our disposal as facilitators is ourselves and our presence. That is of course not to say that the others don't count. It is simply to state that the importance of the preparation, presence, and state of mind of the facilitator is crucial.

As a convener and host of groups, the facilitator influences the space and the group in many visible and invisible ways.

Although much can be planned in advance, a highly skilled facilitator will stay present to what shows up in the moment. For the dialogue to work, the facilitator should not be caught up in a pre-determined structure and timetable that has to be followed at all cost. The rule of thumb: *over-prepared, under-structured*, speaks to the criticality of preparation, coupled with the flexibility to respond creatively as the process unfolds in real time. This may sound like *laissez-faire*, but actually requires great clarity, and the ability to listen to the group and the process. This is where the value of purpose and principles are strongly illustrated: A clear purpose and set of principles that are alive and embodied in the facilitator will enable him or her to improvise and respond with freedom that is rooted in clear direction.

The ability to hold the intentions and principles of a gathering or process clearly and firmly is directly related to how fully present the facilitator is capable of being. Some of the most successful facilitators we know take time for a meditative practice, and time to tune into an intention to serve the group before stepping into the facilitator role. To perform well a facilitator needs to develop humility, but also courage to go with the flow. If the facilitator has this kind of confidence and groundedness, he or she will also gain more legitimacy and trust from the participants.

General qualities of the Dialogue Facilitator:

- *Strong listening skills.* Facilitators need to be able to listen closely during all phases of the process. This enables the facilitator to design an appropriate process, to mirror to participants what is going on and to help the group become more aware. Strong listening skills depend partly on the ability of facilitators to let go of their own agendas.

- *Personal awareness and authenticity.* As much as paying attention to what is going on in the group, good dialogue facilitators need to be able to understand what is going on within themselves when in the group. This is quite a profound meta-skill of facilitation, which is particularly important in less structured, more open-ended processes, and more psychologically oriented processes. Facilitators are essentially holding the group, and need to avoid projecting their own issues and insecurities onto the group while they also deal with projections of the group toward them. Personal awareness relates to the ability to be honest about one's own limitations (what one is and isn't capable of), and the willingness to hand over a process to participants when they are ready.

- *Asking good questions.* As mentioned earlier, in our field, asking good questions is a form of art. Effective questions will wake participants up, link into what they care deeply about, and make visible their interdependence in finding the answers. They will surface new insights participants hadn't thought of before in understanding the issue in focus. A simple phrasing of a question can determine whether people feel hopeless and despairing or curious, energized, strong and excited.

- *A holistic approach.* Being able to assess which method to use in a given situation, or whether one's preferred method is applicable, requires a facilitator to understand the particular context. Taking a holistic approach is also about being able to see patterns, helping the group make connections as they work, and recognizing that multiple intelligences are at work. The more the whole person can be invited in to a dialogue, the more equitably people will be able to engage.

Choosing the right facilitator is crucial. As with the methods, however, your choice of facilitator will depend on the situation. In the following, we have developed four major criteria for assessing facilitators.

A common debate among facilitators is around the question how much a facilitator needs to know about the content the group is discussing. For example, if a facilitator is hired to support a dialogue around HIV/AIDS, does he or she need to know anything about the statistics, who the players in this field are, what the key inter-related issues are or what the politics around the issue are? More broadly, do they need to have a background in the corporate sector or in the development field, if this is the context of the dialogue? Or should it be sufficient that they know how to facilitate a process that enables the participants to process their own information and come to their own answers?

Some facilitators like to know something about the content they are working with so they can help the group find patterns and draw out conclusions, while others believe neutrality and objectivity on the part of the facilitator are fundamental and that deliberate lack of knowledge of the issue in fact helps in this regard. Which type of facilitator you prefer for a specific process will largely depend on whether you feel the group needs support in processing information, or whether they just need their conversations to be supported. This would speak towards a facilitator that does not get too involved with the content.

Directive and structured  **Going with the flow**

Some facilitators will co-design an agenda, usually with the client or group coordinator, and then guide the participants through that process. Future Search or Scenario Processes are examples of methods that are quite structured. The group moves from one phase and exercise to the next, and there is a time limit on each step. The facilitator has to be able to support the group's movement through this process in a specific order.

Other methods require facilitators to literally go with the flow and allow the process to unfold. The idea here is that no one knows in advance what exactly needs to happen for a certain group (least of all the external facilitator). Such a facilitator will come in and will respond to the group's needs, offering methods and approaches that are relevant to the group in the moment. The Sustained Dialogue for example, needs a facilitator who supports the direction in which groups tend to go. Sometimes, the facilitator is drawing on a variety of approaches and helps the group to uncover what it needs to uncover. Again, this approach may be the most appropriate because it is the most adapted to the group's specific needs, but it requires a high degree of trust in the facilitator, and a willingness on the part of participants to engage in an open-ended process.

| No Psychological Expertise | ←——→ | Strong Psychological Expertise |

The issues at the center of a dialogue can be located at different levels. Some are deeply psychological issues, deriving from the relationships within a group that may be related to participants' past traumas or current insecurities. Sometimes facilitators may find themselves in situations that border on therapy. Some facilitators define a clear boundary for themselves emphasizing that facilitation is not counseling or therapy. They will attempt to direct the conversation back to the more content-related issues the group is dealing with. Others see these psychological factors as deeply intertwined with the group's ability to solve everyday problems, and will go into them to try and resolve them.

These are two very different sets of skills. What kind of facilitator you choose depends on whether you feel this group needs to go into its "group unconscious" or whether it needs to focus on more conscious, rational, or practical issues outside of the participants themselves. If a facilitator with a deep psychological expertise comes in, the group is likely to go into that space - sometimes even if they don't want to. If a facilitator is lacking these skills, the group will be restricted from going into it even if they do want to.

Because of the nature of dialogue, all the processes can lead to people going through a fundamental questioning of their core beliefs, which can be unsettling. Deep Democracy is the most psychologically oriented approach described in this book, but the School for Peace approach also benefits from facilitators with psychological awareness. The Circle and Sustained Dialogue can also be processes in which participants open up to a point of significant vulnerability, but in these and the other approaches, therapeutic skill is not necessarily required.

| **Team Worker** | ←——→ | **Solo Worker** |

Some facilitators prefer to work "Solo" because this provides the freedom to improvise and follow their intuition without having to check with partners. Solo facilitators sometimes describe their work as a form of art; they focus on the interplay between them as persons and the group as opposed to wanting to work with a facilitation team.

At the other end of this spectrum are facilitators who prefer to build a team with other facilitators in order to complement each other. The teamwork approach to facilitation can provide a balance between some of the other criteria mentioned in this section. It makes sense, for example, to combine a facilitation team where one is more knowledgeable on process, the other on content, where one is more knowledgeable on societal issues and the other on psychological dynamics, or where one is good at seeing the overall flow of where things are going and the other brings in an expertise in a particular technique. Among Sustained Dialogue practitioners, the prevailing wisdom is that the best moderating teams are "insider/outsider" teams. The insider would be familiar with the content, culture, and personality dynamics of the group, while the outsider brings in process knowledge, and the ability to be objective and ask 'stupid' questions.

Physical Space

Many typical conference-room setups are not conducive to dialogue, but we continue to use them out of habit. We worry more about the agenda, and less about the set-up of the rooms or halls. Meanwhile, the physical space exerts an invisible but incredibly strong influence on what can happen in a process. When people step into a room that is appealing to the senses, something happens to them. It is as if more of the person has been invited in. Before the conversation has even begun, before the intention has been introduced something has already shifted.

The physical space can also hold the collective intelligence of the group as it evolves. It is important to attempt to create these kinds of settings in every single conversation or dialogue process that we initiate.

These questions can help you find the right space:

- Does the space allow for true interaction and participation?

- Is the space a good size for the number of participants?

- Will participants feel comfortable in the space?

- Will the space make us feel relaxed, yet alert and awake?

- Will people meet in this space – in circles, in theater style, board-room style, or around small tables?

- Would it be best to meet in nature, in a coffee-shop, in someone's home?

- Will there be music playing? Refreshments served? How much sound or quiet do we want?

- Are there distractions we might want to eliminate?

II. Tools

We emphasize multiple times through this book that we don't see the tools portrayed in the following as recipes for dialogue that should be applied universally, nor are we prescribing specific tools. We encourage you to read our tool descriptions and to look for the context, story and impetus behind how these processes were developed. A deeper understanding of how processes are designed helps you to design the appropriate process for your own situation.

We do believe that there are underlying archetypal patterns that recur, that conversation is a universal need, and that some of the principles in these methods are deeply human. But it is also important to be aware that we are at risk of falling into the trap of thinking our favorite tool is what will save the world. As mentioned earlier: Tools have an interesting effect on us – they provide safety and comfort, and we become attached to them because they help us to function in a complex world. A tool can become like a lens that affects how we see our surroundings, and if we wear only one lens all the time, our perception of the very thing we are trying to change may become distorted.

This is why we find it useful to continually pose the question of how these different tools and processes can also be combined in new ways. If dialogue itself is about exploration, so should our process be about exploration. The challenge is for us to use these tools wisely to be effective, while being able to hold them lightly and to let them go when they are not serving us any longer. As you read this, we invite you to try with us to find that balance between honoring the energy and the power of these tools, while being conscious that they are nothing more and nothing less than tools.

Method Fingerprint

Exploring the tools in the following chapter, you may be excited about some that you want to experiment with, perhaps nervous or apprehensive about others, or overwhelmed by the variety. How do you decide what method to use in a given situation? How do you perceive whether what is needed is a Future Search, Open Space, Deep Democracy, a Change Lab - or just a contemplative walk in the park?

The intention of this section is to guide your navigation through the variety of options offered on the following pages. However, the reality is that there are no universal recipes informing our choice of tools and there is an infinity of different contextual situations. While there are most certainly good and bad choices for each case, there is never only one ideal method that will guarantee to work.

Experienced facilitators and dialogue conveners will be able to ask exploratory questions to understand the particularities of a situation and to work with the options posed by the different methods. They will develop and continuously redesign a customized process that is not finalized until the process is over because they will be responding to what is happening in the group. On the other hand, a facilitator with such a high level of experiential knowledge, skills, sensitivity and creativity is not always available. For these situations, World Café, Open Space, Circle, and Appreciative Inquiry in particular are great gifts. These processes are more easily applied – even by less experienced facilitators, and they can still make a world of difference. In general, one of the most important points to consider is that the facilitator should be comfortable with the approach chosen. You are better off with a grounded and confident facilitator applying a simple methodology well, than with a sophisticated methodology applied poorly.

In order to provide useful guidance for your selection process, we suggest that you look at a) the *purpose* and b) the *context* of the process you want to design. Please bear in mind that the tool assessment we propose here has clear limitations. We do recommend that you read through the Foundations portion of this book before entering the Tool Section. This will help to ensure that your process is built on the basis of a thorough assessment of the purpose you intend to give the process, the need and the specifities of the participants, the content, process, and physical requirements. The assessment we offer is certainly subjective on our part. Each of the tools *can* basically be used in most if not all of these possible situations, but it would require a creative adaptation or sensitivity on the part of the facilitator, and most likely involve combinations with other methods. However, this rough picture may still help someone who is trying to get an overview and to distinguish between the different tools at a more general level.

The tool portraits are fitted with a method fingerprint displaying our assessment of each tool in relation to both purpose and context. A single ✓ indicates *basic relevance* of the tool, two ✓✓ indicate *appropriateness* and three ✓✓✓ signify an *additional strength* of the tool. For an overview on all tool scorings please consult Appendix A for the overview purpose matrix and Appendix B for the overview context matrix.

Purpose of the Dialogue

In the purpose section of the method fingerprint, we cover possible broad purposes you might be trying to achieve: Generating awareness, problem-solving, building relationships, sharing knowledge and ideas, innovation, shared vision, capacity-building, personal and/or leadership development, dealing with conflict, strategy/action planning and decision-making.

This matrix may be useful not only in assessing what methods work for a given purpose, but perhaps also to provide inspiration in articulating the intentions and objectives of a dialogue. In looking at the purpose matrix, you will notice that the Change Lab for example gets a good score because it meets a large number of purposes, but it is also an intense and high-investment approach. If only a few of these purposes are required, you may well be better off with a simpler approach.

Purpose of the Dialogue Process										
Generating Awareness	Problem-solving	Building Relationships	Sharing Knowledge	Innovation	Shared Vision	Capacity Building	Pers./Leaders. Development	Dealing with Conflict	Strategy/Action Planning	Decision Making

Context of the Dialogue

The context segment of the method fingerprint covers the broader situation of the process, who the participants are, and whether the process requires a facilitator specifically trained for this approach. We considered a few of the situational factors that might vary across methods, including contextual factors, the nature of, and requirements for, participants, as well as the facilitator's level of training.

Context of the Dialogue Process										
Situation				Participants						Facilitation
Low Complexity	High Complexity	Conflictual Situation	Peaceful Situation	Small Group (up to 30)	Large Group	Microcosm/multi-Stakeholder	Peergroup	Diversity of Power Levels	Diversity Of Culture	Specific Training Requirements

- Complexity in the Situation

  The complexity of a process and its context shows in the number and interrelatedness of issues that are connected to the main questions, cause and effect being far apart in space and time in relation to the issue being discussed, a multitude of divergent opinions and interests related to the issue, a constantly changing context, and the fact that old solutions simply no longer work.

  It is worth noting that, as mentioned in the introduction, the evolution of dialogue tools is really in large part a response to increasing complexity, so in fact, all the approaches are intended and specifically designed to be applicable in situations of high complexity. You will notice in the matrix, that we see some of the tools as *exclusively* relevant in such situations, while the rest can also be useful in situations of lower complexity.

- ## Conflict in the Situation

  In defining conflict, we are looking at whether the issue or group is emotionally charged for most of the participants, and whether different, entrenched positions seem incompatible. Is it difficult for people to "agree to disagree"? Are there sub-groups who have conflicts with each other beyond a meeting of individuals, perhaps related to a larger societal conflict? This could include situations where aggression, anger, and attack are taking place – which don't necessarily have to be displayed openly.

  All the approaches may be found useful in conflictual situations if the focus is just on finding common ground despite the conflict, being able to move forward without getting drawn into negativity and stalemate. But if the intention is to go directly into the conflict and resolve it, to release underlying tensions and relationships, and to negotiate a way forward acknowledging the differences, there is a smaller set of approaches that are relevant. If emotions really need to be surfaced and the group is going into its subconscious, we would limit this list even further to Circle, Deep Democracy, Sustained Dialogue and the School for Peace.

- ## Group size

  We picked the number 30 as a useful breaking point between small and large groups. From our understanding, this is where a critical mass of diversity exists, but where the whole group also starts to be constraining and the need emerges to alternate between small groups and the whole. For more specific numbers, consult the tool descriptions.

- ## Systemic Representation

  Several of the processes are specifically designed to "get the whole system in the room", while others are less dependent on this, and can work within a more homogeneous group. Under "microcosm" we have assessed the processes on whether they are designed for reflecting the larger system.

- Diversity of power

  Power dynamics may call for specific requirements in a dialogue process. Can this process work across levels of power and social class? Often participants will be very aware of other forms of diversity such as culture, gender, race, and age, but will not necessarily realize the diversity of power and how power dynamics and hierarchy affect the group. Some of the approaches are explicitly conscious of this impact and include ways of dealing with it.

- Cultural diversity

  Under cultural diversity, we subsume generational, gender, sectoral, and other forms of diversity. As dialogue is always about bridging differences, please note that in the assessment, we have given preference to the tools that are particularly good at this.

- Specific Facilitator Training

  This category looks at whether a facilitator needs to be *specifically* trained to work with the tool. Note that the Circle, Open Space, World Café, and Appreciative Inquiry are the most accessible for beginner facilitators to use. They are like instruments that can sound beautiful even the first few times you play them, but it is still possible to grow increasingly more sophisticated and effective in one's use of them as experience is gained. We have also not checked Future Search in this category because we felt a person with strong facilitation skills does not necessarily need specific Future Search training, though they do need to be a strong facilitator.

Appreciative Inquiry

Overview

Appreciative Inquiry (AI) is an approach and process which turns problem-solving on its head. Instead of finding the best ways to solve a pressing problem, it places the focus on identifying the best of what's already present in an organization or community and finding ways of enhancing this to pursue dreams and possibilities of what could be.

Appreciative Inquiry originates in the work of David Cooperrider. As a doctoral student in 1980, Cooperrider made a shift in his approach in research at the Cleveland Clinic. He was studying the factors that contributed to the organization's health and excellence. Recognizing the power that the change in focus from problem to positive resources brought about, he began to lay the first foundations for what is today Appreciative Inquiry. He worked under the guidance of his advisor Dr. Suresh Srivastava, and the encouragement of clinic leaders who were seeing the potential of his approach for more widespread organizational development.

Problem Solving	Appreciative Inquiry
• "Felt need" & identification of problem • Analysis of causes • Analysis of possible solutions • Action planning • Assumes: Organization is a problem to be solved • What's in the way of what we want?	• Appreciate & value the best of What Is • Imagine: What Might Be • Dialogue: What Should Be • Create: What Will Be Assumes: Organization is mystery to be discovered • "Front Door": what is it we ultimately want?
Deficit Thinking	**Possibility Thinking**

A key underlying assumption of this approach is that the questions we ask strongly influence the answers we find. Questions that can elicit strong positive responses can be more powerful in driving people towards a positive future. This approach allows people to work towards something that is energizing and inspiring instead of overcoming something that is deficient and dysfunctional. Appreciative Inquiry uses these findings to improve social systems, organizations and communities. Appreciative Inquiry is by its nature a cooperative process that collects, builds on, and works with the strengths, life-giving forces and "good news" stories that are found in any community or organization.

The AI Process steps

- Select focus area or topic(s) of interest
- Conduct interviews designed to discover strengths, passions, unique attributes
- Identify patterns, themes and/or intriguing possibilities
- Create bold statements of ideal possibilities ("Provocative Propositions")
- Co-determine "what should be" (consensus re: principles & priorities)
- Create "what will be"

The AI process

As the diagram below shows, there are four main steps to the AI process. Before working through this depiction of the "four D's" of AI, there comes an initial step of defining the focus of inquiry. Doing this collaboratively is an incredibly important point of departure. As the below diagram shows, there are four main steps to the AI process. Before working through this depiction of the "four D's" of AI, there comes an initial step of defining the focus of inquiry.

Doing this collaboratively is an incredibly important point of departure. And it is important to frame it as an affirmative topic, and not a problem statement. For example: "creating and sustaining high-quality cross gender work place relationships," is an affirmative topic, whereas "cutting incidents of sexual harassment" is a problem statement.

Discovery – Appreciating and valuing the best of what is. This is a system-wide inquiry (through interviews and storytelling) into people's experience of the group, organization or community, at its most vital and alive, reflecting on those highlights and clarifying what made those experiences possible. This is also known as identifying the positive core of a system. This phase includes clarifying those elements that people want to keep even as they (their organization, community) change in the future, as well as identifying intriguing potentials for the future.

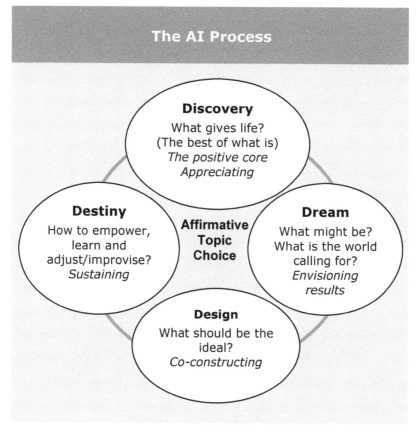

The AI Process

Discovery
What gives life?
(The best of what is)
The positive core
Appreciating

Destiny
How to empower,
learn and
adjust/improvise?
Sustaining

**Affirmative
Topic
Choice**

Dream
What might be?
What is the world
calling for?
Envisioning
results

Design
What should be the
ideal?
Co-constructing

Dream – Envisioning *what might be*. Together people build a vision of a future they want. They respond to their sense of what the world is calling them to become. They imagine that the best of *what is* forms the foundation for the way things will be in the future. Questions in this phase include: *What does our positive core indicate that we could be?*, *What are our most exciting possibilities?*, *What is the world calling us to become?*

Design – In this phase, people determine *what should be*, crafting an organization or community in which the positive core is vibrant and alive. The design focus is placed on elements that can help bring the dreams to life, such as practices, structures, policies, technologies, etc. The work is to develop provocative propositions (bold ideal possibilities) and principles of design that integrate the positive core.

The four guiding principles in AI

- Every system works to some degree; seek out the positive, life-giving forces and appreciate the best of what is.

- Knowledge generated by the inquiry should be applicable; look at what is possible and relevant.

- Systems are capable of becoming more than they are, and they can learn how to guide their own evolution – so consider provocative challenges and bold dreams of "what might be."

- The process and outcome of the inquiry are interrelated and inseparable, so make the process a collaborative one.

(Source: Appreciative Inquiry, An Overview – compiled by Kendy Rossi)

Destiny – This final phase takes the step towards creating the initiatives, systems or changes needed to make real the future as articulated in the design propositions. This phase can be done using Open Space (see section on Open Space later in this document) to make the most of the creativity and insight of the people involved, and allowing self-selected groups to plan the next steps in the areas that they are most passionate about, and willing to take responsibility for. (See separate section on Open Space Technology).

The full process can be organized in what is called an AI summit, including several hundreds people coming together for 2-6 days. In an AI summit, the first phase (Discovery) always kicks off with personal interviews around several questions that elicit stories of highlights and strong positive experiences. This is followed by people working in smaller groups and teams, to map patterns and distil the positive core from the stories. Together they continue into envisioning "what might be" together, followed by co-constructing "what should be." In each of these phases there is continuous feedback to the whole, to enable the whole system to integrate what is happening in other groups.

Applications

Appreciative Inquiry can be used in several ways – one is using an AI summit as described above, where an organization, community or any system comes together for 2-6 days to go through the full AI process with the aim to engage in a large scale change or developmental process. It could be strategic planning,

Ap-pre'ci-ate (verb):

valuing; the act of recognizing the best in people or the world around us; affirming past and present strengths, successes, and potentials; to perceive those things that give life (health, vitality, excellence) to living systems;

to increase in value, e.g. the economy has appreciated in value

In-quire' (kwir) (verb):

the act of exploration and discovery

to ask questions; to be open to seeing new potentials and possibilities

community development, systems change, organizational redesign, vision development, or any other process in which there is a genuine desire for change and growth based on positive inquiry, and for allowing the voice of people at all levels of a system to be heard and included.

Although this application can be seen as an isolated process, it is very much based on a way of being where organizations or communities can co-create a desired future building on the best of the past. The AI summit is often simply the beginning of a continuous process of examining and building on strengths and possibilities. These can include anywhere from 50 – 2000 people.

Secondly, Appreciative Inquiry can also be done as an on-going process of interviews and dialogues that take place throughout a system (organization, community, and city). The case below is an example of such a process.

Finally, the principles of AI can be integrated in simple yet powerful ways in most workshops and other gatherings, following its basic principle of asking appreciative questions, and working with storytelling as a powerful agent to engage and involve people. A simple guideline is to learn the art of asking appreciative questions that elicit compelling stories, and questions that help envision the future.

Case Example – The Imagine Movement

Imagine Chicago is part of a movement of imagination. It considers itself as a catalyst in this movement, supporting the sprouting of Imagine initiatives on six continents. While each Imagine effort is distinct, all the efforts share a few common convictions: that human beings can unite around shared meaning; that each person's contribution is vital to a flourishing community; and that creating a culture of public learning and civic engagement that connects generations and cultures is at the heart of self- and social transformation.

'For the twenty years we have been in Chicago, we have only been talking in our community organization about survival. Now we have been asked what we have to contribute to the city. It is an exciting question that we are now asking ourselves.'

Participant of 'Imagine Chicago'

Bliss Browne, the founder of Imagine Chicago, began in 1993 with a vision inspired by conversations with many well-known city pioneers and social innovators (the following text is partly excerpted from 'Imagine Chicago – Ten Years of Imagination in Action,' written by Bliss W. Browne and Shilpa Jain). She began to imagine a city where every citizen, young and old, applies their talents to create a positive future for themselves and their community, where hope comes alive in the flourishing and connecting of human lives, where young people and others whose visions have been discounted, develop and contribute

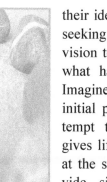

'Human System grow toward what they persistently ask questions about'

David Cooperrider and Diana Whitney

their ideas and energy. In seeking ways to bring the vision to life, she created what has today become Imagine Chicago. The initial project was an attempt to discover what gives life to the city, and at the same time, to provide significant leadership opportunities for youth, who most clearly represent the city's future. During 1993-1994, the Imagine Chicago team initiated two parallel pilot processes of intergenerational civic inquiry as the starting point for a broad-based conversation about the future of the city of Chicago. They were: 1) a city-wide appreciative inquiry, and 2) a series of community-based and community-led appreciative inquiries.

The citywide interview process involved approximately 50 young people as interviewers. They interviewed about 140 Chicago citizens who were recognized by the Imagine Chicago team as "Chicago glue," including artists, politicians, business and civic leaders, and other young people. Over a period of many months, deep, one-on-one conversations took place between the adolescents and adults about the city's past and about visions of its future. Both youth and adult participants later described these conversations as "energizing," "rejuvenating," and "transforming."

In the community-based pilots young leaders interviewed local community-builders across different ethnic communities. All of the pilot interview projects broadened the participants' views of what was possible, both within themselves and within the city. The stories conveyed in these small group interviews were shared in a series of civic forums where Chicago citizens convened and began devising projects to bring about positive change in specific neighborhoods and public institutions. The appreciative questions were clustered around three main stages of appreciative inquiry, which still today is the common organizing structure for all of Imagine Chicago's initiatives. This approach moves from idea to action in a generative cycle, which borrows its inspiration from the basic structure of appreciative inquiry:

Understand what is (focusing on the best of what is) - All of Imagine Chicago's work begins with and is grounded in asking open-ended and value-oriented questions about what is life-giving, what is working, what is generative, what is important.

Imagine what could be (working in partnerships with others) - New possibilities are inspired by interesting questions or stories, which stretch our understanding beyond what we already know.

Create what will be (translating what we value into what we do) - For imagination to lead to community change, it needs to be embodied in something concrete and practical, a visible outcome that inspires more people to invest themselves in making a difference.

Imagine Chicago intergenerational interview questions:

1. How long have you lived in Chicago? In this community?
   a. What first brought your family here?
   b. What is it like for you to live in this community?
2. When you think about the whole city of Chicago, what particular places, people or images represent the city to you?
3. Thinking back over your Chicago memories, what have been real high points for you as a citizen of this city?
4. Why did these experiences mean so much to you?
5. How would you describe the quality of life in Chicago today?
6. What changes in the city would you most like to see?
   a. What do you imagine your own role might be in helping to make this happen?
   b. Who could work with you?
7. Close your eyes and imagine Chicago as you most want it to be in a generation from now. What is it like? What do you see and hear? What are you proudest of having accomplished?
8. As you think back over these conversations, what images stand out for you as capturing your hopes for this city's future?
9. What do you think would be an effective process for getting people across the city talking and working together on behalf of Chicago's future?

Imagine Chicago supports the creation of initiatives and programs in partnership with local organizations and institutions. All three processes feed into and out of each other; the interdependent relationship enables them to transform individual and community visions into realities.

Commentary

Appreciative inquiry is particularly effective with people who have been disempowered and are focusing too much on their deficiencies. It is an important contrast to the common approach of seeing people as "poor" and in need of "help" from the outside. A general tendency in "development work" is to focus on deficiencies, survey needs, and seek to solve problems. Not only does this mean we overlook some opportunities, but this approach also has a negative impact on the self-esteem and creativity of people involved.

We have used Appreciative Inquiry with rural people in Zimbabwe, and there has been an amazing impact as they begin to operate from a clearer and stronger sense of the wealth and wisdom they have as a community. When they discover that they can harness their own resources in various forms, they become able to break out of a scarcity and dependency mindset, which in turn generates a sense of freedom,

Resources

Barrett, Frank, and Fry, Ron (2005). Appreciative Inquiry: A Positive Approach to Building Cooperative Capacity

Cooperrider, David, Diana Whitney, and Jacqueline Stavros (2007). Appreciative Inquiry Handbook

Cooperrider, David and Diana Whitney (2005). Appreciative Inquiry: A Positive Revolution in Change

Whitney, Diana, Amanda Trosten-Bloom and David Cooperrider (2003). The Power of Appreciative Inquiry: A Practical Guide to Positive Change

http://www.appreciative-inquiry.org

http://www.imaginechicago.org

and possibility, as well as creativity and self-esteem. Their ability to imagine and plan for the future comes from an entirely different place of strength and vision. Appreciative Inquiry in this context is related to other development tools such as the "community asset map" and "ca-pacity inventories". On the other hand, Appreciative Inquiry can focus so entirely on the good, that it prevents a full view of a situation, and becomes illusory. It can also feel restrictive, as if only the positive is allowed in, and conflict is not allowed to surface.

Our experience has been that when we bring in an appreciative approach it needs to go hand in hand with releasing what has been painful, or feels limiting. This could for example be by complementing it with circle dialogue, deep ecology work, scenario exercises or other tools. This is especially the case when working more intimately with a community over an extended period of time. Working appreciatively should not be about closing our eyes to the things we don't want to see. Finally, Appreciative Inquiry is a great exercise in becoming aware of our questions and the impact that questions have on human thoughts and actions.

Category	Item	Rating
Purpose	Generating Awareness	✓✓
	Problem Solving	✓
	Building Relationships	✓✓
	Sharing Knowledge	✓✓
	Innovation	✓✓
	Shared Vision	✓✓✓
	Capacity Building	✓
	Pers./Leadersh. Dev.	✓✓
	Dealing with Conflict	✓
	Strat./Action Planning	✓✓✓
	Decision-Making	✓✓
Situation	Peaceful Situation	✓✓✓
	Conflictual Situation	✓
	High Complexity	✓✓
	Low Complexity	✓✓✓
Participants and Facilitation	Small Group (≤ 30)	✓✓✓
	Large Group (≥ 30)	✓✓✓
	Multi-Stakeholder	✓
	Peergroup	✓✓✓
	Div. of Power Levels	✓
	Div. Of Culture	✓✓
	Specific Facilitation Requirements	✓

Change Lab

Overview

The Change Lab is a multi-stakeholder dialogic change process. It is designed to generate collective insight, shared commitment, and creative capacities needed to address complex social problems. Each Change Lab is convened by one or more organizations that are committed to effecting change in relation to a certain complex problem, and aware that they cannot solve this problem alone. The conveners bring together 25-35 key stakeholders of the issue who somehow represent a "microcosm" of the system, in that they reflect the diversity of players involved in producing and addressing the problem. These people need to be influential, diverse, committed to changing the system, and also open to changing themselves. The Change Lab process which these stakeholders move through together, is built up around three major movements or phases:

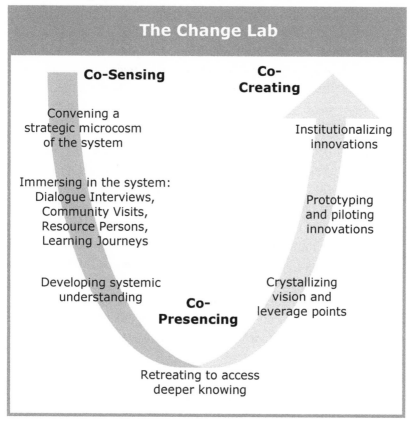

The Change Lab

Co-Sensing

Convening a strategic microcosm of the system

Immersing in the system:
Dialogue Interviews,
Community Visits,
Resource Persons,
Learning Journeys

Developing systemic understanding

Co-Presencing

Retreating to access deeper knowing

Co-Creating

Institutionalizing innovations

Prototyping and piloting innovations

Crystallizing vision and leverage points

Co-Sensing, Co-Presencing, and Co-Creating. This process draws inspiration from the "U-Process", a creative social technology, co-developed by Otto Scharmer and Joseph Jaworski. It has been further developed drawing on the multi-stakeholder process work of Adam Kahane as well as a wider community of practitioners. It continues to evolve as more experience is gained and shared.

Change Lab Phases

Each of the phases of the Change Lab is associated with a set of different leadership capacities, activities, and tools.

- In the *Co-Sensing* phase, the participants transform the way they perceive the problem. They are trained in, and practice, different ways of seeing and perceiving, so that they are not just projecting their pre-conceived ideas onto the problem. They work with understanding each other's perspectives, motivations, and frames of reference through dialogic interviews with each other. They immerse themselves in the situation by going on learning journeys to visit affected and involved communities and organizations. They share their stories and try to create maps of the system. They look at their own dynamic as a microcosm of the system. They surface their shared body of knowledge, and formulate the 'problem space' and the 'solution space' in multiple iterations.

- In *Co-Presencing*, the participants usually spend time in silence. The Co-Presencing aspect of the Change Lab often involves a "wilderness solo", a reflective period of time spent alone in nature. This is a powerful practice to enable the capacities of presencing: letting go and letting come. While the Co-Sensing experience may have overwhelmed them with complexity, the Co-Presencing experience is about creating emptiness, allowing "inner knowing" to emerge, connecting to what really matters, and in that process finding a new simplicity. In focus is uncovering shared purpose and connecting to their deeper will: what do they each deep down want to do about this issue?

- In the *Co-Creating* phase, the participants crystallize insights in terms of the basic characteristics that need to define a new system as well as creative ideas for solutions. These ideas are now translated into "prototypes" – "mock-up" versions of the solution that can be tested first with the Lab Team and then with a wider group of stakeholders. The prototyping process is about going beyond writing up the idea in a document to trying to create an experience of the initiative for people. It is also about taking a more emergent approach which allows a constant adaptation of the initiative in conversation with the context. This is in contrast to a more traditional approach where the activities of planning and implementation are separate in time and space. The prototyping approach enables team members to build, test, improve, and re-test interventions in the real world.

Innovations which, on the basis of this prototyping, hold the greatest promise for effecting systemic change, are then developed further into pilot projects. Finally, these pilots are scaled up, mainstreamed, and institutionalized with support from committed government, business, and civil society partners.

Applications

The Change Lab is intended to address problems that are complex in three ways:

- *Dynamically*: cause and effect are far apart in space and time, resulting in the need for a *systemic* solution;

- *Generatively*: the future is unfamiliar and undetermined, and traditional solutions aren't working, resulting in the need for an *emergent* solution;

- *Socially*: no single entity owns the problem and the stakeholders involved have diverse - potentially entrenched and antagonistic - perspectives and interests, resulting in the need for a *participative* solution.

Because of the level of complexity being addressed and the scope and scale of these problems, the full Change Labs are often run over a period of several years requiring investment of significant time, attention, and financial resources. However, it is possible to run shorter and condensed versions of a few days to a few months, and still have a remarkable impact, and it is also possible to do it both at local and global levels. There is no one recipe for running a Change Lab, and there are many practitioners around the world experimenting with different ways of facilitating innovation drawing inspiration from the underlying model of the U-Process.

If you are trying to run a larger Change Lab, and you want to convene a microcosm of a system across sectors, it is important to be aware of whether parties from all the sectors and major stakeholder groups are willing to be involved. If the key actors needed in order to construct a "microcosm" of the system cannot be convened and committed, the Change Lab may not be the right approach.

Case Example: The Sustainable Food Lab

[Excerpted from the SFL website at http://www.sustainablefoodlab.org]

The intention of the Sustainable Food Laboratory (SFL) is to create innovations that make food systems more economically, environmentally, and socially sustainable — in other words, profitable and affordable, in balance with nature, and good for producer and consumer communities. The initial 35 members of the SFL Team first gathered at a "Foundation Workshop" in the Netherlands in June 2004. Together they made up a microcosm of the stakeholders in global food supply chains: farmers, farm workers, processors, wholesalers, retailers, consumers, representatives of government agencies, activists, financiers, researchers and others. The group, which has since grown to 70 members, primarily consists of participants from Europe and the Americas. Each of the team members was invited because of their proven track record as an innovator, their on-the-ground experience combined with a bird's-eye perspective of food systems; and their passion, entrepreneurship, and influence.

When the SFL was launched, each of the team members was frustrated by what he or she had been able to accomplish working only in his or her own organization and sector. In joining the Lab, they initially committed to 40 days or more of work over two years, in whole team workshops, learning journeys and sub-team work on prototype and pilot projects.

Through the SFL, they are now engaging in dialogue and action to achieve changes more ambitious than they could achieve separately.

The Process: After the Foundation workshop in the Netherlands, each Lab Team member went on one of three five-day learning journeys in Brazil. When they had returned from and synthesized the results of their journeys, the whole team reconvened for a six-day Innovation Retreat including a wilderness solo. Out of the Innovation Retreat, the members made choices about initiatives to start working on in sub-teams. At a subsequent meeting in Salzburg in April 2005, they proto-typed the new initiatives, which are now being piloted and institution-alized while the group continues to meet periodically.

SFL Systems Map

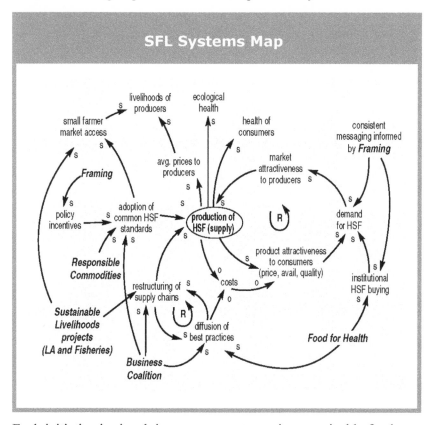

Each initiative is aimed, in some way, at creating sustainable food sup-ply chains and bringing them into the mainstream. The six initiatives that came out of the Salzburg gathering are:

1. Linking sustainable food production from Latin American family farmers to global markets

2. Delivering high-quality nutrition from regional farmers to schools and hospitals

3. Building a business coalition for sustainable food

4. Creating sustainability standards for food commodities and related investment screens for food companies

5. Re-framing food sustainability for citizens, consumers, and policy makers

6. Increasing the sustainability of fish supply chains

The diagram above reflects the link between these initiatives and the overall map constructed by the SFL team to illustrate the linkages in the food system. It is still early to document the results of the SFL initiatives, but it's clear that the Lab has generated new thinking, new relationships and strong partnerships across sectors, and has started shifting the global food system both by changing the participants and through the initiatives they are now busy carrying out.

Commentary

The Change Lab has some key distinguishing strengths:

1. *The approach is systemic.* Throughout the Change Lab, participants are building "system sight". They are defining the problem space and solution space in a systemic way, and as a microcosm of the system, they are also a reflection of the wider issue.

2. *It is action-learning.* The Change Lab is a dialogic process and has dialogue embedded in it throughout. But it is also an action process. It doesn't stop at the point where new ideas or insights have been generated. The Lab Team stays together through piloting the new initiatives and continues to relate these initiatives back to the picture of the whole system, so the effort doesn't become fragmented.

3. *The Change Lab is a process, more so than a tool.* It draws on 20 years of experimentation with different kinds of tools and

integrates the best ones in various phases. The theme, pattern, and glue that hold these different tools together are the Change Lab process, inspired by the U-Process. This also means that the Change Lab is very flexible and can adapt around that core pattern.

There are a number of risks and challenges involved in convening a Change Lab as well. Working with stakeholders from a diversity of organizations and sectors and coordinating the different interests involved can slow the process down significantly. This can be exacerbated because the process is unfamiliar to many, and some of the practices may lead to resistance. In some cases, it helps to start with a "mini-Lab" – a 3-day miniature version of the Change Lab – to give participants a sense of what a larger process could achieve.

If you are trying to run a larger Change Lab, and you want to convene a microcosm of a system across sectors, it is important to be aware of whether parties from all the sectors and major stakeholder groups are willing to be involved. If the key actors needed in order to construct a "microcosm" of the system cannot be convened and committed, the Change Lab may not be the right approach.

Category		Rating
Purpose	Generating Awareness	✓✓✓
	Problem Solving	✓✓
	Building Relationships	✓✓
	Sharing Knowledge	✓✓
	Innovation	✓✓✓
	Shared Vision	✓✓
	Capacity Building	✓✓
	Pers./Leadersh. Dev.	✓✓
	Dealing with Conflict	✓
	Strat./Action Planning	✓✓✓
	Decision-Making	✓✓
Situation	Peaceful Situation	✓✓
	Conflictual Situation	✓✓
	High Complexity	✓✓✓
	Low Complexity	✓
Participants and Facilitation	Small Group (≤ 30)	✓✓✓
	Large Group (≥ 30)	✓
	Multi-Stakeholder	✓✓✓
	Peergroup	✓
	Div. of Power Levels	✓✓
	Div. Of Culture	✓✓
	Specific Facilitation Requirements	✓✓

Very importantly, Change Labs, even short ones, tend to be resource-intensive. It usually takes a great deal of effort to get all the right stakeholders in the room and to coordinate the process, and it costs money to organize learning journeys, wilderness retreats, and innovation workshops, and to support the action phase of the Change Lab. In situations of low complexity, or where the purpose is purely to share knowledge or build relationships, a full Change Lab would generally not be worth the effort and other tools would be more appropriate and sufficient. The purpose really needs to include a need for innovation and shifts in awareness and capacity, the context needs to be complex, and the group needs to be multistakeholder in order to justify the choice of a Change Lab.

Resources

Senge, Scharmer, Jaworski and Flowers (2004). Presence: Human Purpose and the Field of the Future

Scharmer, Otto (2007). Theory U.

Kahane, Adam (2005). Solving Tough Problems.

http://www.sustainablefoodlab.org

http://www.ottoscharmer.com

http://www.generonconsulting.com

http://www.reospartners.com

http://www.dialogonleadership.org - Documentation of a series of rich and in-depth interviews with innovators in this field, conducted primarily by Otto Scharmer

The Circle

Overview

For as long as humankind has been around, the circle has been with us. Human beings have naturally been gathering in circles, around the fire, in deep conversation, sometimes in the quiet space of simply being together. At its most essential level, the circle is a form that allows a group of people to slow down, practice deep listening, and truly think together. When practiced fully, it can be a physical embodiment of the root of the word dialogue: "meaning flowing through".

Imagine a circle of elders, passing a talking piece around one by one. Everyone's attention is on the person currently holding the piece, sharing his or her thoughts, perspectives, and wisdom. Each person's voice is valued and honored. Long pauses of silence are an accepted part of the conversation.

People can come together regularly over periods ranging from a few months to several years in the circle, or they can meet in a circle as a stand-alone gathering. In recent years, the Circle is having a comeback in different variations. From business executives in corporate boardrooms to community organizers in rural hinterlands, people are re-connecting with the value of sitting in a circle.

Many of the processes described in this collection make use of circular meeting forms in one way or another because it is generally the most suitable configuration for a dialogue. This section, however, looks specifically at the Circle as a process method, not only as a physical set up.

The three principles of the Circle

- Leadership rotates among all circle members. The circle is not a leaderless gathering - it is an *all leader* gathering.

- Responsibility is shared for the quality of experience.

- People place ultimate reliance on inspiration (or spirit), rather than on any personal agenda. There is a higher purpose at the centre of every circle.

Here, we draw on the guidelines developed by Christina Baldwin of PeerSpirit. Inspired by her exploration of Native American traditions, Baldwin wrote a book entitled "Calling the Circle", which has made a major contribution to re-introducing circle process and developing a set of practices that can help us to facilitate meaningful circle dialogues. These guidelines can be used in their entirety or held more lightly.

Intention

As with most of the tools and processes of good dialogue, the starting point is with the purpose and intention. The intention will determine who should be invited to join, when, where, and for how long they will meet, as well as what questions they will focus on.

The clearer the intention and the stronger the commitment to it, the stronger the circle. There are leadership circles, where people gather to support each other in their respective leadership practice. There are also circles that come together to solve a specific challenge such as improving a program in an organization, or working together to make a neighborhood safer. It could be a group of workers coming together in circle with management to find the best way to deal with a need to retrench people, or even a group of homeless people joining members of a local church congregation to together come up with the best ways to support the homeless.

Sometimes a circle is simply a tool used in a larger process during the course of a workshop, or as a weekly or monthly meeting in an organization, or community. In this case the intention is more informal – to share expectations, to connect with how each other is doing, and to surface and address any concerns or needs people may have.

The host

Although leadership is fully shared in circle, there will always be a host for the particular circle. Often the host is also the caller of the circle, but where a circle meets continuously over a longer period of time, the host role can change from circle meeting to circle meeting. The host will ensure that the circle flows through its main phases and that the intention is at the centre of the dialogue. The host is often also responsible, with the "guardian" (see below), for the actual physical space.

Special attention is paid to the physical centre of the circle – a colorful rug, some meaningful symbols or objects, and/or a plant may mark the centre of the circle and often represent the collective intention. This paying attention to the centre of a circle, brings with it a sense of the sacred, when people gather together around it.

The Guardian

The Guardian is the person who pays special attention to the energy of the group, and that the group is not straying from the intention. The Guardian may interrupt during the course of the circle to suggest a break or a moment of silence.

Flow of a typical circle

Welcome. The welcome helps the group shift into circle space. A good welcome can be a poem, a moment of quiet, or a piece of music to help people fully arrive, and to become present to each other and their circle.

Check-in. One thing that distinguishes a circle from many other ways of coming together is the importance placed on bringing each voice into the room. The circle therefore begins with a check-in where each person has a chance to speak to how they are feeling, as well as sharing their expectations for the meeting that day. The host may pose a specific question for each person to respond to in the check-in. It is also not unusual to invite participants to place an object representing their hope for the circle in the centre, sharing a little about the object as they do so. The result is a meaningful visual representation of the group's collective hopes in the center.

Agreements. When any circle gathers, its members need to formulate guidelines or agreements on how they wish to be together. This is an important part of shared leadership and everyone taking responsibility for their time together.

Farewell/Check-out. At the end of a circle, similar to the check-in at the beginning, there is now a check-out for people to share where they are at. The focus of the check-out can be as diverse as each circle.

It can be on what people have learned, how they are feeling about what emerged, or what they are committing to do moving forward from the circle. Every participant usually speaks in the check-ins or check-outs unless they explicitly choose not to.

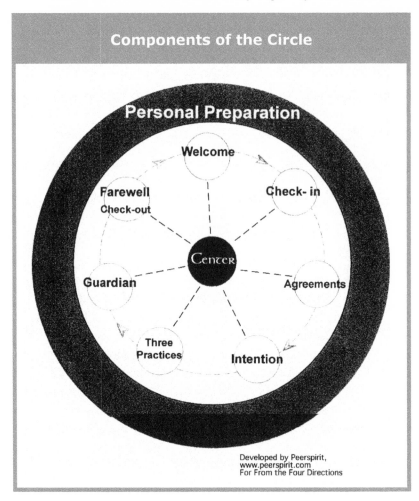

Components of the Circle

Personal Preparation

Welcome

Check-in

Agreements

Intention

Three Practices

Guardian

Farewell
Check-out

Center

Developed by Peerspirit,
www.peerspirit.com
For From the Four Directions

Forms of Council

The circle is well known for the use of the talking piece. The talking piece is passed around the circle, with the person holding it being the only one to talk. The talking piece can be anything – an object from nature, a photograph, a pen, or even a mobile phone. However, the talking piece is not a necessary feature of the circle. Often the check-in is done with a talking piece, but then people can move into talking without it.

This version is also called conversation council, where anyone who has something to say speaks. When people have been using circle for a while, even in conversation council, the practice is ingrained to not interrupt someone, and to let each person finish before a new person begins. Sometimes conversation speeds up a little too much in the Circle, and the centre – or calm – gets lost. This is where the Guardian, or anyone who feels the need, can call the circle into reflection, or silent council, where everyone is silent for a while, letting things settle, before continuing either with the talking piece or in conversation council.

Examples of commonly used agreements

- Listen without judgement

- Offer what you can and ask for what you need

- Confidentiality – whatever is said in the circle, stays in the circle

- Silence is also part of a conversation

Three Practices

Essentially the circle is a space for speaking and listening, reflecting together and building common meaning. Three practices have been clarified, which can be useful to help people come into a higher quality of attention:

- Speak with intention: noting what has relevance to the conversation in the moment.

- Listen with attention: respectful of the learning process of all members of the group.

- Tend the well-being of the circle: remaining aware of the impact of our contributions.

Applications

As mentioned earlier, the Circle is the most fundamental form of humans organizing for joint conversation, and in that sense, it is of course used all over the world, and has been for millennia. Christina Baldwin's work in particular also has a global reach. She has done trainings in Europe, North America, and Africa, and frequently emails "Peer Spirit Tales" of how the circle is being used in different settings. An initiative launched in collaboration with the Berkana Institute, called "From the Four Directions" led to the launching of numerous leadership circles in North America, Europe, and, to a lesser degree, beyond.

The Circle is good for:

- Building relationships and enabling a group to connect more intimately

- Creating equality among people who are at different levels in a group, organization or community – giving equal value to each person, and requiring everyone to participate

- Slowing people down and allowing them to think together and build shared vision

There is a lot of power in using the circle for a group meeting over a period of time, but it is also valuable to bring depth to a process or workshop by including circle check-ins and reflections during the course of the gathering.

In our experience, up to 30 people (max 35) should be in a circle together. With 8-15 people one is able to go much deeper. It can also be used in larger processes, breaking the group into several circles. For this, it does need someone familiar with the basics of The Circle to facilitate each group initially.

Case Example – Kufunda Village

At Kufunda Village – a learning centre focusing on rural community development in Zimbabwe – the circle has become a core part of the work with communities as well as the way the centre itself is run. Every time the centre does its evaluations of its programs, or of the work in the communities themselves, the circle comes up as a key factor of success. People seem to connect fully with it, perhaps because it is a part of the traditional culture. At its simplest, there is a daily morning circle during community programs in which each person checks in with how they are feeling around the program, key learnings that survived the night and hopes and expectations for the day.

The effect of using the circle with rural community organizers is that, where it might typically have been primarily adult men who would contribute, here everyone speaks. Slowly but surely, they build the confidence and naturalness

> 'Round the fire was where conversation took place. Every evening we would sit around the fire, and talk.'
>
> Silas, Kufunda Village

of each person to contribute fully to everything that is done together. At the end of several programs, men express their surprise at how much they have been able to learn in honest conversation with women (in the Shona system women and men often confer separately), or the elders from youth.

The circle is taken back home to the communities that Kufunda works with, and it has become a natural way of meeting for all of the partner communities, allowing for the voice of the youth and the Chief alike to be expressed. At Kufunda, a monthly team retreat day, where circle is used a lot (though not only) brings the team together in a more intimate way, giving space for people to express and work through concerns, needs or new ideas that may not make their way to the group during daily business. Each team at Kufunda, meeting weekly, begins and ends all their meetings with a talking piece check in and check out. It means that people don't dive straight into business, but allow themselves to arrive and connect with each other, before getting into work. The check-out usually allows for reflection on how people are feeling about what was covered or decided. In times when the team struggles with misunderstandings, dedicated circle work has been invaluable in clearing the air – through a practice of truth-telling, choosing to listen without interrupting and jumping into defense. These are all aspects which the circle help promote. Another example of a powerful use of circle is in the Alcoholics Anonymous (AA). Essential to the AA model are weekly meetings of alcoholics to be in dialogue and reflection together, bearing witness to each person's challenges and progress. At these meetings people can ask for help with personal problems in staying sober, and they get this help from the experience and support of others like them. There is no hierarchy, rather it is a place to create a community of support for people who all share a desire to stop drinking and stay sober. It is a place where people can show up as who they are, letting their masks down, and not needing to hide their fear. There are open and closed AA meetings. The closed meetings are the ones that most resemble circle as we've described it here. The relationships and capacities people build at AA often turn out to be lifelong and relevant in a much broader range of situations.

The following list is a reflection on what the circle means both to Kufunda's employees and community partners from a series of evaluations done.

- The circle brings a sense of belonging
- Everyone contributes
- Everyone is a leader
- People speak from the heart
- Silence is ok
- It takes you out of your comfort zone
- It disrupts hierarchy
- It connects people
- It is intimidating
- It is liberating
- Everybody's voice is heard
- It is effective in conflict
- The circle is regulated by guidelines created by the group
- It fosters equality

Commentary

If the group is too large to form one circle, but you still want every-one's attention on one impor-tant conversation, one useful approach can be to use the "fishbowl", or what is known as "Samoan Circles". Here, participants are divided be-tween an inner circle and an outer circle, with only the in-ner circle speaking and the outer circle listening. The in-ner circle can either be repre-sentative of the whole group, or of a sub-grouping, and sometimes it is set up so that people can move in between the inner and outer circles. This process is particularly useful when issues are contro-versial, or if the group is too large to fit into one single cir-cle.

For many who are not used to the circle, the slowness of the conversation and thinking can be frustrating. With time most people learn to value and ap-preciate the gifts of slowing down together, to really listen to each other. Generally, peo-ple who tend to be less vocal and less powerful will appre-

Purpose	Generating Awareness	✓✓
	Problem Solving	✓✓
	Building Relationships	✓✓✓
	Sharing Knowledge	✓✓
	Innovation	✓✓
	Shared Vision	✓✓✓
	Capacity Building	✓
	Pers./Leadersh. Dev.	✓✓
	Dealing with Conflict	✓✓
	Strat./Action Planning	✓
	Decision-Making	✓✓
Situation	Peaceful Situation	✓✓✓
	Conflictual Situation	✓✓
	High Complexity	✓✓
	Low Complexity	✓✓
Participants and Facilitation	Small Group (≤ 30)	✓✓✓
	Large Group (≥ 30)	✓
	Multi-Stakeholder	✓✓
	Peergroup	✓✓✓
	Div. of Power Levels	✓✓
	Div. Of Culture	✓✓✓
	Specific Facilitation Requirements	✓

ciate the circle immensely because they are given the space to speak, while those who are used to dominating a conversation will be more frustrated.

It's worth noting that Social Science research shows that the first person to speak can have a large influence on what is said and the direction the conversation takes. The circle seems particularly prone to this dynamic. This can be useful, but it can also be problematic. The way around it is to give people time to reflect in silence and collect their own thoughts before people start to speak. In general, the host should be aware that while the circle has a great equalizing influence on a group, informal power dynamics still exist, and can influence the conversation.

Resources

Baldwin, Christina (1994). Calling the Circle: The First and Future Culture.

http://www.peerspirit.com

http://www.fromthefourdirections.org

Deep Democracy

Overview

There are a variety of reasons why people in a group may not be saying what they really think. Perhaps it is considered taboo, politically incorrect, or too sensitive, or they may just feel that they will never actually be heard and able to influence the majority view of the group. *Deep Democracy* is a facilitation methodology which is based on the assumption that there is a wisdom in the minority voice and in the diversity of viewpoints, which has value for the whole group. The approach helps to surface and give expression to what is otherwise left unsaid.

Deep Democracy was developed by Myrna Lewis in South Africa with her late husband Greg Lewis based on 15 years of intense work in the private and public sectors. It is closely related to, and draws on, Arnold Mindells' process-orientated psychology and "worldwork", but offers a more structured and accessible set of tools.

Picture an iceberg. Generally, only 10% of the iceberg is above the waterline, while 90% is concealed in the depths of the ocean and not visible. Many psychologists use this as a metaphor for the conscious and unconscious of human beings. Only a part of what drives us is conscious while the bulk of it is unconscious. Similarly, in a group coming together for some purpose, there are aspects that are conscious to the whole group and aspects that are in the *group's unconscious*. The group's unconscious will often be reflected in the one-on-one and small group conversations that happen outside the formal meetings, in hints and jokes, in the excuses people make for being late or not doing what they were supposed to, and in unexpressed emotions and opinions.

Much of our work is comfortably done above the surface in the realm of the conscious. But sometimes there are underlying emotional dynamics that continuously block us from moving forward, from solving a problem or coming to a decision. In this situation, Deep Democracy is designed to bring these issues to the surface and facilitate their resolution. The idea is that the group's highest potential and wisdom is hidden in the depths and will be brought out by surfacing what is in the unconscious. If issues in the group's unconscious have built up over time because of a lack of open communication, the group may have to go through a conflict process to release them. Conflict here is seen not as something to be avoided, but as an opportunity for learning and change. The earlier a conflict is expressed and spoken about in the open, the less painful it will be.

A key aspect of Deep Democracy is that the process focuses on roles and relationships rather than on individuals. We normally think of "roles" as social roles, jobs, or positions. In Deep Democracy, a role can be anything expressed by a person, for example, an opinion, idea, emotion, physical sensation, or an archetypal role like the parent/the child, the teacher/the student, the oppressor/the victim, the helper/ the needy, and so on. A role is usually held by more than one individual, and an individual usually holds more than one role in the group. The most personal is linked to the universal, in that each person actually deep down has the capacity and potential to express any role. S/he has both an individual identity as well as access to the overall pattern and knowledge of the whole.

A system will tend to be healthier if roles are fluid and shared. If one person is alone in a role, it becomes a burden to that person. If roles are too fixed, the organization or group isn't growing. In Deep Democracy, the role of the facilitator is to help people make the roles more fluid, to become aware of themselves, each other, and their interdependence, and through that to access their wisdom. The facilitator is trying to help the group to *lower the waterline* of their iceberg.

The first four steps

There are five steps to Deep Democracy. The first four make up a unique approach to decision-making and take place *above the water-line*:

- *Don't practice majority democracy.* Traditional majority democracy will take a vote and then move forward with a decision. But the idea that the minority will just go along happily with the majority decision is actually a myth. In Deep Democracy, the decision with a majority vote is not the end point. The minority voice is encouraged to express itself. Don't settle for the vote.

- *Search for and encourage the "no".* The facilitator needs to make it "safe" for people to express their dissent, and not feel afraid to say "no". The minority view is encouraged and given permission to speak.

- *Spread the "no".* Once the "no" has been expressed, other participants are asked if they agree with the "no" even if only in part. People are encouraged to express agreement with the "no". This process avoids scapegoating and people being singled out and ostracized for disagreeing.

- *Access the wisdom of the "no".* When the majority has decided to go in a certain direction, the minority is asked "what do you need to go along with the majority?" This is not a second chance for the minority to say "no". The minority will add wisdom and elaborate on the decision by qualifying it with what they need to come along. This helps the group come to a more conscious decision.

This decision-making process is an unusual attempt to get a decision where the minority actually comes along and buys into a decision. It looks like a consensus but is not exactly the same. In many situations this decision-making process will be enough, if there is not too much baggage or underlying conflict behind the decision. If decisions are taken in this way, the minority will feel heard, the group will be more conscious about why it's doing what it's doing, and conflicts will be settled early before they become painful.

Below the waterline

Sometimes it is not enough to stay above the surface. When resistance to a decision continues, when people keep having the same small arguments, when they start *sounding like a broken record*, when they feel unheard, or are being very indirect, there is a need to go "under the waterline", and move into the 5th step of Deep Democracy. This is done through a process whereby the facilitator *turns up the volume* on a conversation. When a participant speaks in a way that is indirect, the facilitator goes in and speaks for that person, amplifying what they are saying, making it more direct and taking out the politeness.

 The facilitator in effect becomes an instrument for the group. The participants talk directly to one another, rather than talking at the facilitator. The facilitator is making the message clear and direct, which gives people something to respond to. Ideally, she is not adding meaning, but literally speaking on the participant's behalf. It's like putting an electrical charge on the words, and looking for a reaction from other participants. Participants are always made aware that they can correct the facilitator if she gets it wrong.

In order to do this amplification, the facilitator needs to apply a set of *metaskills* - attitudes and behaviors with which the facilitation skill or tool is used. The two most important ones are neutrality and compassion. The facilitator needs to not be judging what people are saying as good or bad, and to really support people in the totality of their experience. This can for the facilitator require a lot of "inner" work on his/her own personal awareness, so that he/she can come into the group centered and still conscious of his/ her own baggage.

If the discussion becomes polarized through the amplification, the group may decide to actually go into a conflict. This is always made as a very conscious agreement, and participants are told to remember that the purpose of the conflict is growth and about remaining in relationship. It is not about winning a battle. In a Deep Democracy conflict, all participants agree to express themselves fully and to *own their own side* completely. This is different from many other forms of conflict resolution where participants are encouraged to focus on trying to understand the *other* side or point of view first.

During the conflict, the participants are explicitly requested not to express defensiveness, but must take turns getting everything off their chest. When a conflict starts to be resolved, you generally find that the different sides start saying the same thing. They become more silent and contemplative. At this point, each participant is requested to share at least one personal learning – a grain of truth that they have received from the conflict. The wisdom from these grains of truth is taken back to the initial issue the group was trying to resolve.

Applications

Deep Democracy is a relatively young process, but is spreading quite rapidly. In South Africa it has been used in corporate settings as well as in schools, with HIV/AIDS counselors, and in youth groups. Myrna Lewis is currently training Deep Democracy facilitators from a number of countries including the UK, the US, Denmark, Israel, France, Ireland, and Canada.

The key strength of Deep Democracy is in recognizing the important role that emotional dynamics can play and in incorporating wisdom into decision-making. Deep Democracy is most useful in situations where: things are unsaid and needing to be brought into the open; people are stuck in roles and conflict may be arising; there is a diversity of views in a group, and different sides to an issue need to be considered; power differences are affecting people's freedom to act; there is a need to gain the buy-in of a minority; and/or, people are being labeled by others.

Case Example – Immigration in Denmark and the Topic of Honor

Immigration is currently one of the most politicized problems in Denmark. As an issue, it is having an impact on how elections fall out, and not a day goes by when it is not covered in the news. In particular, there is an emphasis on the conflict between the Muslim culture of many immigrants and the mainstream Danish culture.

'Immigration is such a burning issue for us in Europe and this was the first time I experienced an honest and open conversation about the issue where everything that needed to be said was said and we were all stronger for it.'

Participant

In May 2005, a group of 20 people gathered in Copenhagen, Denmark to learn about Deep Democracy. About a quarter of the group were non-Danish residents, while the rest were Danish citizens, half of whom were ethnically Danish and the other half second-generation immigrants or of mixed ethnicity. The group was asked by the facilitator to make a decision together on what they would like to talk about. Two participants self-selected to facilitate the decision-making process. One of them started by immediately saying he wanted to speak about the issue of "honor". He was working with youth of an immigrant background and found that they often justify violence with an excuse that someone has breached their honor. He wanted to understand what that was about and how to deal with it to stop the violence. Participants "cycled" around wanting or not wanting to discuss this topic. One person, a non-Dane, said that the issue of honor was entirely irrelevant to him in his work. Another person suggested that the group should rather discuss immigration issues, seemingly unaware that the honor question was at the very heart of immigration issues.

It was the moment when someone personalized the issue, sharing that he had felt a breach of honor in relation to another participant, the group decided to go into a facilitated conflict. Through the conflict, some participants gained awareness of their own racism and privilege while others became aware that they had been in a victimhood mentality and not taking responsibility. It turned out that some of the immigrant participants felt that the Danes had left honor behind generations ago and didn't understand why honor was important in Muslim cultures. Part of what was striking about this process is that Danish culture has in the past been, and seen itself as, very generous towards immigrants. The space in which immigrants could be allowed to criticize Danish culture, and speak openly about their concerns is never created partly because this would be perceived as being ungrateful.

Following the conflict where both sides had been allowed to speak their mind, each participant owned a "grain of truth". The following day, there was a deep understanding towards each other in the group, and a sense of joint endeavor and desire to collaborate around working to improve the cultural clashes in the broader society.

Commentary

Deep Democracy is obviously quite an unusual process. We are used to trying to avoid or contain conflict, polarization, and disagreement. Instead Deep Democracy invites it in,

Purpose	Generating Awareness	✓✓✓
	Problem Solving	✓✓
	Building Relationships	✓✓
	Sharing Knowledge	✓
	Innovation	✓✓
	Shared Vision	✓
	Capacity Building	✓✓
	Pers./Leadersh. Dev.	✓✓
	Dealing with Conflict	✓✓✓
	Strat./Action Planning	✓
	Decision-Making	✓✓✓
Situation	Peaceful Situation	✓✓
	Conflictual Situation	✓✓✓
	High Complexity	✓✓
	Low Complexity	✓✓
Participants and Facilitation	Small Group (≤ 30)	✓✓✓
	Large Group (≥ 30)	✓
	Multi-Stakeholder	✓✓
	Peergroup	✓✓
	Div. of Power Levels	✓✓
	Div. Of Culture	✓✓
	Specific Facilitation Requirements	✓✓✓

and at times even provokes it. The result, when this process works at its best, is a lively openness and transparency and a very powerful strengthening of relationships and collaboration. Participants may go through a process where a large part of the time is spent in discussion that is antagonistic and polarizing, and yet feel afterwards as if they have experienced a deep heartfelt and empathetic dialogue.

It's important to recognize that when Deep Democracy encourages conflict, it is based on an assumption that conflict is already present and actually inevitable. But sadly, conflict is often contained until it is too late to do anything about it or for it to be resolved peacefully. The idea here is to try to bring it on as early as possible so that it will be less painful and explosive and more generative and transformational. This is done by helping people to express themselves honestly to each other through the facilitation tools of the five steps.

In our view, it's vital to have a well-trained and experienced facilitator when working with Deep Democracy, especially in groups where the stakes are high. This is probably the tool in this collection which takes the most in-depth training to be able to facilitate, and it is never mastered completely. Even with a good facilitator, Deep Democracy is usually at first a frustrating experience for participants. This is part of the experience, but it just makes it all the more important that the facilitator is confident and clear on what they are doing and why.

The value of Deep Democracy in relation to dialogue facilitation is as much the philosophy and assumptions behind it as the specific tools. There are some simple tips from Deep Democracy thinking which are useful for any group dialogue process. In particular, we find the idea of "spreading the no" and not letting participants get stuck in a role very useful. Rather than following the tendency of answering criticism and singling people out in a group, invite the critical voice in by asking if anyone else shares that viewpoint. When there is dissent to the direction in which a group is going, ask "what would it take for you to come along?"

Resources

http://www.deep-democracy.net

Future Search

Overview

Future Search brings the "whole system" into the room to look at the past, present and future experiences of participants, through a task-focused agenda. The design is based on the intention to have all participants take ownership of this past, present and future, thereby finding common ground for collective future action. A Future Search conference has a specific theme, which all stakeholders work on over a 3-day process. An important principle of the process depends on all the participants accepting an open invitation to spend a few days together in an explorative process.

Future Search was designed by Marvin Weisbord and Sandra Janoff as a process where diverse groups of people with a stake in a community or organization can plan their future together. They have written a book called Future Search which explains the process in detail, and is summarized in this short overview. A Future Search process has a specific structure to follow, which has been designed and evolved based on the experience of hundreds of similar gatherings. The process would typically bring together 60-70 participants. This number works on the principle of bringing the "whole system" into the room, by selecting at least 8 stakeholder groups, who are equally represented by approximately 8 participants each.

The Process

The Future Search process recommends that the agenda includes at least 2 "sleep-overs", and spans over three days. A typical Future Search agenda would look as follows:

Day 1, Afternoon (1-5pm)

Focus on the past: Mixed groups sit, share life stories and discuss milestones which they have experienced over a specified number of years. Each person from these groups then plots their experiences on massive flipcharts on the walls, which have been divided into categories of society/self. The end result will be a long row of experiences which have filled flipcharts on the wall. This gives everyone in the room a sense of the collective past experiences, and the parallels between individual trajectories and societal trajectories.

Focus on present, future trends: The whole group together now reviews trends which currently affect our lives and communities. These experiences are documented by the facilitator onto a "mindmap". After these have been put onto the mindmap, participants are given stickers of colored dots to "vote" which trends they feel are most important. The session ends here, and gives participants the opportunity to reflect on this overwhelming diagram of complexity overnight.

Example of Mindmap with sticker dots

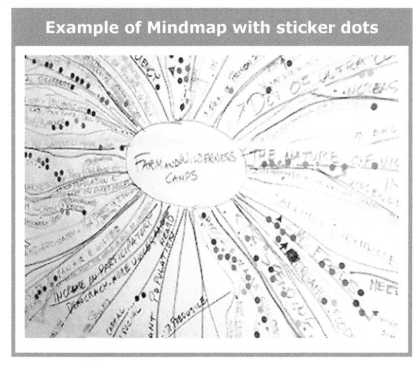

Day 2, Morning (8:30am-12:30pm)

Continued – trends: The larger group is now divided into their stakeholder groups (around similar interests/context). These stakeholder groups review the trends and decide which ones are important and which they want to take ownership for.

Focus on present, owning our actions: Each stakeholder group then discusses which of their group's contributions to these trends they feel proud of or sorry about.

This is where each stakeholder group takes personal responsibility for the current issues at hand. The groups present their "prouds" and "sorries" to the bigger group, which relates to the trends they have been prioritizing.

Day 2, Afternoon (1:30-6pm)

Ideal future scenarios: The group returns to their mixed groups from the day before. The purpose of this exercise is to imagine their desired future 10-20 years from now, and act out this scenario to the bigger group as if it is happening today. It is important to encourage the groups to think with their minds, bodies and emotions, tapping into unconscious aspirations. They also need to highlight which barriers they overcame from the time of the Future Search up until the time of the scenario.

Identify common ground: Once these scenarios have been acted out, the mixed groups highlight what the common future themes are that have emerged. They also look at potential projects or strategies which will help them get to these futures. Finally, they note what disagreements still remain.

Day 3, Morning (8:30am-1pm)

Continued – confirming common ground: The whole group reviews the lists from the previous afternoon. A discussion is facilitated to try to understand what each statement means, and whether or not there is agreement. If there is no agreement, then it is noted, and the group moves on. This exercise also explores the tension between the actual and the ideal. The group needs to decide whether they want to use the limited time remaining to delve further into the conflict areas or focus on the common ground already created.

Action-planning: Participants now have the opportunity to invite others interested in a particular project or theme to join them in action-planning. This process is similar to "Open Space", explained in a separate section, and the purpose is to encourage people to work across boundaries in addressing these themes. These groups then report back, highlighting how this information will be implemented and disseminated, and then the conference is closed.

Preparation for a Future Search

The preparation process of a Future Search conference is the key to the success of the meeting. Getting all the stakeholders taking ownership of the meeting, as well as attending, is a process which takes time. A Future Search is usually "sponsored" by a particular organization or person (sometimes a key stakeholder), who pulls together the other stakeholders, and "hosts" the preparation.

Applications

Future Searches have been used extensively around the world, on every continent. Countries include Sudan, Russia, Sri Lanka, Botswana, Sweden, Northern Ireland and Australia. It has also been used within different sectors such as healthcare, education and business. An extensive overview of applications is available on the Future Search website.

According to Weisbord and Janoff, the conditions required for a future search session to be successful include:

1. *The "whole system" needs to be in the room.* Future Searches only work if "the whole system" is in the room. It is critical that as many key stakeholders of an issue are present in the room and that the different voices of a "whole system" are contributing. Diverse perspectives allow new relationships to be built, and a stakeholder can learn more about itself and the world by interacting with other con-

It is recommended that at least 2 preparation meetings be held with a representative from all stakeholders present to do the following:

- define the purpose and expectations
- introduce facilitators
- agree on program
- decide on an invitation list
- organize logistics

stituencies. If there is only part of the story being told by a group of people who normally interact with each other, a collective future cannot be envisioned, and a Future Search can't work.

2. *The "Big Picture" as context to local action.* To get participants on the same wavelength, it is important to get everyone talking about the same world. Therefore it is important for the group to describe this world in as much detail as possible before doing anything about it. The conference therefore starts by exploring the "global trends".

3. *Exploring current reality and common futures, not problems and conflicts.* Future searches delve into future scenarios, rather than problem-solving or conflict management. The process acknowledges differences, but does not work through them, as the purpose of the meeting isn't about team-building or conflict resolution. Common ground is the backdrop for planning in this process.

4. *Self-managed explorations and action plans.* Self-managed groups are used throughout the process, reducing passivity, hierarchy and dependency on facilitators. The intention is to shift control from external facilitators. Small groups are recommended to rotate roles of facilitator, reporter and timekeeper.

5. *Attending the whole meeting.* It is important that every participant be involved in the shifts which change their perspective on what needs to be done, and to build common ground. For this to work, everyone needs to be there for the whole meeting. It is also discouraged to have non-participants or observers present.

6. *Meeting under healthy conditions.* As has been highlighted in the introduction to this toolkit, good food and a healthy atmosphere with natural light help people's energy and ability to concentrate. The space should be easy to move around and have the flexibility to change for small or large groups, with lots of wall space for flip-charts.

7. *Working across 3 days.* It is not the amount of time which is important, but the space to absorb the learning over 2 nights which is a benefit. It is assumed that the unconscious works on unfinished business overnight, which is how the program is designed.

8. *Taking responsibility publicly for follow-up.* Having people select the action groups they sign up for and to publicly acknowledge their next steps helps to share ownership and commitment to the follow-up process.

Case Examples

The following cases are adapted from Weisbord,/Janoff: *The Future Search book, 2000.*

Nation-building in Bangladesh. UNICEF agreed to sponsor a Future Search training in Bangladesh, a country with a population of 110 million people, and many social challenges. The intention was to train local facilitators who would in turn host future searches to envision new realities for Bangladesh's future, and move the largely poor population out of poverty. In 1994, 50 Bangladeshi consultants, trainers and managers came together for the training. One of the challenges was that participants struggled to envision large future dreams, for example, a country without child labor. The participants agreed that "we need to learn how to dream". A number of follow-up conferences were planned, and future searches were run on topics including "Stopping Children with Diarrhea from Dying", "Early Childhood Development", "Child Labor", "Stopping the Spread of HIV/AIDS", and others. These conferences have proved to be very popular as planning tools in Bangladesh, and have subsequently spread to other parts of South East Asia, including Nepal, Pakistan and Sri Lanka.

Regional Economic Development: the Inuit People, Canada. When the Inuit people of the Artic region were granted a new homeland, they embarked on a Future Search to develop a strategy for economic development. The Future Search process was conducted in both the local language and English, and included drum dancing and other traditional features. The conference included a range of stakeholders of the newly formed homeland, and produced frameworks for education and training, social development, preservation of culture and language, small business development, transportation, infrastructure and other organizational aspects of action-planning. The Inuit people have sponsored several subsequent future searches, and local community leaders have learnt the future search techniques of facilitating community-based planning at many local levels.

Commentary

A Future Search is a structured process with a sophisticated meeting "architecture" that has been consciously designed to flow in a particular order. This is a strength, but it can also appear too rigid. It's important to realize that while the instruction on how to do a Future Search may seem to imply that there is only one way to do it, the Future Search website and newsletter include active discussions among practitioners who have adapted it in various ways to different cultural contexts. There is clearly some variety in how it is applied.

One of the aspects of Future Search which we find most powerful is its use of visual techniques and creative processes. The history timeline which the group puts together on the first day across an entire wall usually tells a strikingly complex story, as does the colorful mindmap of current trends. Similarly, the challenge to people to act out their scenarios of the future rather than just drawing them up on a flipchart invites in multiple intelligences and invokes imagination.

Purpose	Generating Awareness	✓✓
	Problem Solving	✓✓
	Building Relationships	✓✓
	Sharing Knowledge	✓✓
	Innovation	✓✓
	Shared Vision	✓✓✓
	Capacity Building	✓
	Pers./Leadersh. Dev.	✓
	Dealing with Conflict	✓
	Strat./Action Planning	✓✓✓
	Decision-Making	✓✓
Situation	Peaceful Situation	✓✓
	Conflictual Situation	✓✓
	High Complexity	✓✓✓
	Low Complexity	✓✓
Participants and Facilitation	Small Group (≤ 30)	✓
	Large Group (≥ 30)	✓✓
	Multi-Stakeholder	✓✓✓
	Peergroup	✓
	Div. of Power Levels	✓✓
	Div. Of Culture	✓✓
	Specific Facilitation Requirements	✓✓

It is important to note what Future Searches cannot do. For example, Future Searches cannot make up for weak leadership. If leadership doesn't act on the ideas from a Future Search, or buy in to the process, it will not work. This process stops at the point of action planning and leaves the implementation as the responsibility and ownership of the stakeholders participating. Future Searches also cannot reconcile deep value differences. If people disagree deeply based on religious or political differences, it is unlikely to be resolved in a Future Search. Future Search quite explicitly chooses to put disagreements aside and focus on commonalities. In many contexts this is sufficient but if underlying issues or disagreements will block action, it may need to be replaced or complemented by other processes.

Finally, great facilitation trainings are available for Future Search, but we also feel that if one has strong general facilitation skills, it is possible to be able to facilitate a Future Search based on the excellent written material available in the book and on the website.

Resources

Weisbord, Marvin and **Sandra Janoff** (1995, 2000). Future Search:An Action Guide to Finding Common Ground in Organizations and Communities.

http://www.futuresearch.net

The Israeli-Palestinian School for Peace

Overview

In 1972, a group of Arabs and Israelis came together to create a village where they would live together voluntarily. They called this village "Neve Shalom" / "Wahat El Salam", which means "Oasis of Peace" in Hebrew and Arabic. In 1976, the community founded a School for Peace which was to create encounter programs for Jews and Arabs, drawing on the community's rich experience of living together. They believed that if they could just bring Jews and Arabs together in a real personal encounter, the dominant stereotypes would be reduced, and peace would become possible.

Today, the founders recognize that they began with a naïve outlook. They soon discovered that the "contact hypothesis" – the idea that all you need to do is to meet and get to know the other - doesn't actually fare well empirically. If you just bring people together and enable them to become friends, what happens is that they simply manage in their mind to separate their new friend from his/ her group. The attitude is essentially, "You are ok, you can be my friend, but you're not typical, you're not like all the other Jews/ Arabs/ black people/ white people…" This mental rationalization is called "sub-typing".

The Israeli-Palestinian conflict is a conflict between two peoples, rather than between individuals. The School for Peace team realized that stereotypes are just a symptom, revealing deeper conceptions that are hard to eradicate. Collective identities are real, and constructed by stable and deep-rooted beliefs. Contrary to some theories, they are not easy to educate away, or to buy off with economic development.

Based on this reality, the School developed a more sophisticated and critical approach to encounter programs. They set it up as an encounter between two national identities, and started encouraging participants to identify with their group. Today's approach was developed through trial and error, and only gradually and in hindsight did they find more and more social science theories supporting it.

The Process

The intention with the programs is to allow participants to examine their own identity through the encounter with the other group in authentic and direct dialogue. It is really around creating awareness and understanding, enabling participants to comprehend the turbulent and violent processes taking place all around them in Israel, and their own role in the conflict. The School creates a safe space that allows participants to examine their feelings and thoughts in a group. They critically examine things ordinarily taken for granted, challenge the existing reality, and pose new possibilities

Each of the programs involves equal numbers of Arabs and Jews as participants, and equal numbers of Arab and Jewish facilitators as well. The groups are usually divided into small groups of approximately 16 participants – 8 Arabs and 8 Jews, with one Arab and one Jewish facilitator assigned to each group. Both Arabic and Hebrew are official languages and participants are encouraged to speak in their mother tongue with translation. The facilitators' role is to clarify the processes, to analyze and mirror back to the group what is going on, and to create links to the external reality in ongoing dialogue with the participants.

The groups meet in two fora: the bi-national encounter group (Arabs and Jews together), and the uni-national group (Arabs and Jews meeting separately). The participants usually spend about 3/4 of the time in the encounter group and 1/4 of the time in their uni-national group. At first, participants tend to criticize the introduction of the uni-national group. They don't see its value given that they have come together in order to meet across cultures. But as the conversations become more conflictual, the uni-national group becomes a safer place where they can feel free to be vulnerable, to examine their own identity, to share deep realizations, and also to explore sub-identities within their group. These sub-identities include for example the difference between Muslim, Christian and Druze Arabs, and between Ashkenazi (European) and Mizrahi (Middle Eastern) Jews or liberal and nationalist Jews. It is harder to examine these differences in the bi-national encounter group because the Jewish-Arab line of identity is what is prominent there.

Purpose	Generating Awareness	✓✓
	Problem Solving	✓✓
	Building Relationships	✓✓✓
	Sharing Knowledge	✓✓✓
	Innovation	✓
	Shared Vision	✓✓
	Capacity Building	✓✓
	Pers./Leadersh. Dev.	✓✓
	Dealing with Conflict	✓✓✓
	Strat./Action Planning	✓
	Decision-Making	✓
Situation	Peaceful Situation	✓
	Conflictual Situation	✓✓✓
	High Complexity	✓✓
	Low Complexity	✓
Participants and Facilitation	Small Group (≤ 30)	✓✓✓
	Large Group (≥ 30)	✓
	Multi-Stakeholder	✓✓
	Peergroup	✓✓
	Div. of Power Levels	✓✓✓
	Div. Of Culture	✓✓
	Specific Facilitation Requirements	✓✓✓

'In awareness, however painful, is embodied one of the most human values: the right to have a choice, and the option to change and be changed.'

Rabah Halabi

The topics that are central to the inter-group dialogues are around inequities, Israeli politics, cultural dynamics, and the experience of being Jews and Arabs in Israel. The participants are invited to bring up topics that they find interesting or troublesome. The idea is that for social change to happen, a real, genuine, and eye-to-eye dialogue needs to happen between these two groups. In order for the two groups to come together at an equal and authentic level though, the facilitators have found that the Arab group in every process has to first become strong, to shake off their inferiority, and uproot their internalized oppression. If they can build a clear, confident, aware, and demarcated in-group identity, they are better equipped to conduct inter-group dialogue.

The groups at the School for Peace are assumed to be a "microcosm". This means that even though they are not demographically representative, all the elements of the larger society may be found in some form in each person and each group. The facilitators at the School believe that the process that unfolds over and over again in these groups reflects the path the overall society is on, and the journey Israel as a country needs to go through. The actual process may differ depending on the program. We provide two examples below – a university program and a youth program.

Applications

So far, the School's programs have been attended by 35000 people from different walks of life – from attorneys to activists, schoolchildren to teachers. Through these programs, they have not only impacted the individuals participating but also their friends, colleagues, and families. They also teach courses at Israel's main universities.

We are not aware of the extent to which the approach has spread and been replicated in other countries. The situation in Israel and Palestine is of course extreme, but many of the dynamics that show up sharply in this process are archetypal dynamics common between minority groups and powerful majority groups. The process seems highly relevant to racial, ethnic, or other minority-majority dynamics in different contexts, and aspects of it even to dialogues between sectors, generations, or other kinds of groupings.

Case Examples – Adult and Youth Programs

Adult Programs: The university program described here took place at Tel-Aviv University in 1996-97. A group of 16 students, half Arab half Jewish, met over 22 sessions of 3 hours each. The group went through five phases, typical of these programs.

1. *Initial explorations and declarations of intent:* In this first phase, the participants were being polite and cautious and the group boundaries were unclear. Each group was identifying with members of the other group, and the discussion was focused on the nature of the encounter.

2. *Strengthening one side:* Now, one side of the group started to solidify and unite, showing courage, and drawing strength from each other through the uni-national meetings. They would express differences in the uni-national meetings but not in front of the other group. The groups started sitting separately and expressing their identity more clearly. One group started dominating, focusing on demanding rights, and criticizing the other group.

3. *Resumption of power by the other side:* The other group experienced a loss of control and power. They didn't know how to cope with the unfamiliar, strong identity of the others. They expressed frustration and despair and considered leaving the program. They started now joining the victim position, pointing out how the others were reversing the roles, and alluding to their lack of sensitivity and humanity. "We understand you, but you don't understand us." A struggle ensued over who is more humane. One group regained control by targeting the other group's weak

spot. Now they feel distressed, and the others felt they were back in control.

4. *Impasse:* Both sides were exhausted and despairing. The dialogue felt as if it had been wrung dry. Then, one person started speaking to the choices facing them. Despair shifted to action, and out of a sense of lost cause emerged a different depth of dialogue. Both groups accepted the balance of power and met the other "eye to eye".

5. *A different dialogue:* One group owned up to their own sense of superiority and became willing to talk about themselves as rulers and the strong group. There was a sense of breakthrough and mutual respect. The humanity of both sides was restored as both the "oppressed" and the "oppressors" were liberated within this microcosm. The group identity became less central again and participants returned to being individuals. The dialogue returned to practical questions around how to live together and how to return to reality.

Youth Programs: The Youth Programs are the most common programs at the School for Peace. These are four-day programs, more structured than the adult programs, and not quite as psychologically intense as what is described above.

In the youth programs, usually about 60 eleventh-grade students aged 16-17 come together and divide into four groups of 14-16 people who work in parallel through the four days.

1. *The first day* is focused on getting acquainted personally and easing anxieties. A comfortable and optimistic atmosphere is created. Participants introduce themselves, learn each other's names and the significance of their names, talk about familiar topics such as school, home, and future plans, and share personal stories in pairs.

   The focus is on what they have in common. Games and activities help to break the ice, and an exercise is introduced that can only be solved through collaboration across cultures. Political discussions are avoided. The power relations are still present however, in that the Jews will tend to be most vocal and everyone is speaking Hebrew.

2. *The second day* they start getting to know each other's cultures. In mixed groups of 4, they are given cards with discussion topics about cultural differences. The conversation starts being about "the way we do…" and "the way they do…". Here the dialogue transitions from interpersonal to inter-group dialogue, and the youth start coming face-to-face with their feelings of superiority and inferiority. After a uni-national meeting, they come back into an encounter session that now starts to broach politics through a "photo-language" exercise.

   Participants are asked to select a photo from a collection, and use it to describe how they feel as an Arab/Jew in Israel. Through the visualizations picked and talked about, each side is able to express their emotions. Thus, each side is struggling to justify its own narrative. The day ends in uni-national meetings. Here, both sides realize that it was the first time many of them have been required to really engage and argue with the "other" side.

3. *The third day* is run as a simulation game. The youth are asked to imagine that 50 years into the future there is a comprehensive peace between Israel and the Arab states but the status of the Arab minority within Israel hasn't changed. Demonstrations happen, and the Israeli government opens up negotiations with the minority around: security, education, symbols and representation, and the character of the state.

   The youth now have to create negotiating teams for each of these four topics and imagine that they are in this political process. They struggle with whether it is just a game, or whether it is reality. They are challenged to really figure out what they stand for and what kind of society they want.

4. *The fourth day*, they have a closing dialogue and talk about how to take their lessons home. Each participant writes a letter to be copied for all the others in an album to remember the experience, and each is given a certificate of attendance in a celebratory ceremony.

Commentary

The School for Peace approach is surprising and contrary to much of what we have been taught about dialogue. What attracts us to it, and leads us to include it in this book, is its emphasis on authenticity and facing up to reality, and developing a process that is not imported from a different context, but truly applicable to Israel.

Most, if not all, of the other methods in this collection emphasize strongly that individuals have to speak for themselves, and that being a representative of a group or organization inhibits dialogue. Here, the centrality of collective identity is not ignored but incorporated. Many of the other tools profiled in this book have been developed by people of privileged backgrounds: Like no other tool, the School for Peace helps understand the perspective of minorities and disempowered groups. However, the School for Peace approach is difficult and complex, and participants can feel it is not respectful of individual differences and allowing personal expression.

To us, including this approach is not so much a suggestion of replicating it as a whole, but more to consider the questions it raises about the difference between individual and group encounters, and to incorporate aspects of it in other processes where groups are coming together and power differences are present. In particular, it may be worthwhile in many inter-sectoral, inter-cultural, or inter-generational groups to allow participants to move between groups that are diverse and groups that are more homogeneous.

Resources

Rabah Halabi, Ed. (2004). Israeli and Palestinian Identities in Dialogue: The School for Peace Approach

http://sfpeace.org

Open Space Technology

Overview

Open Space Technology allows groups, large or small, to self-organize to effectively deal with complex issues in a very short time. Participants create and manage their own agenda of parallel working sessions around a central theme of strategic importance. What Open Space presents to us is, at the very least, a new way to hold better meetings. It can however grow to become a new way of organizing that infuses entire organizations or smaller communities.

Harrison Owen initiated Open Space Technology in the mid 1980's. He had had several experiences of good to great conferences where the real highlights were the conversations outside of the formal agenda. This led him to wonder whether a different way of organizing might not be possible. His question moving forward became how to combine the level of synergy and excitement present in a good coffee break with the substantive activity and results characteristic of a good meeting.

> 'With Open Space, there are no ideas that remain hidden or unspoken. Everything emerges.'
>
> Open Space practitioner

In seeking for answers, he took some of his inspiration from witnessing a four-day long rite of passage for young men in a West African village in Liberia. Though there was seemingly no organizing committee or formal structure, the four days ran smoothly with all 500 people managing themselves, the activities, events, food, music, and all the other aspects of the ceremonial process. From this experience, Owen took some of the fundamental principles that have come to shape Open Space today. In brief they are: the circle as a centre from which organizing takes place; a breath, or rhythm, that people know and can organize around; the village market place where connections are made around different offerings; and the bulletin board, where information is posted and shared.

Open Space has since become the operating system beneath some of the largest self-organizing meetings the world has seen. The benefit of Open Space is that people get involved in contributing, and working through, the areas that they are truly engaged in and committed to. The danger (to some) is that freedom is given to people to choose their response and involvement without being controlled by a planner or organizer.

How it works

An Open Space meeting can last from two hours to several days. When people gather they co-create the agenda of the meeting together, allowing it to be shaped by the passion and interest of the people. Every Open Space meeting begins in a large circle. One facilitator is all that is needed. After an initial welcome, she will open the space, by introducing the theme, or burning question, which has brought people together. She explains that within the next hour, their agenda will be formed on the large seemingly very blank wall. She explains that all of the sessions will be posted and hosted by the participants themselves. People are invited to propose sessions and discussions on topics that they themselves are passionate about and willing to take responsibility for, in response to the theme or question at the centre. But before beginning the collective agenda-making, the facilitator still needs to explain the basic principles and one law of Open Space.

Four Principles

- *'Whoever comes are the right people'.* This principle speaks to people to let go of their need to have certain specific people join their group. Perhaps they would like the people in certain positions of influence or the experts in an area. With this principle people are invited to acknowledge that those who care enough to freely choose to join a conversation are the best ones to initiate work in that area.

- *'Whenever it starts is the right time'.* This principle recognizes that while a session may begin at a certain hour, creativity and inspiration don't always work according to our desired timing. Things really get started when they are ready.

- *'Whatever happens is the only thing that could have'*. This invites people to let go of expectations for how and where things should go. We need to learn to let go of these expectations and instead be present and pay attention to what is actually happening and emerging among us.

- *'When it's over, it's over.'* We don't know how long it takes to deal with an issue. In Open Space, the issue is more important than the schedule. If we finish before the allotted time is over, then we move on to something else. We should not stay somewhere just because the schedule tells us to. It also works the other way. If we have not finished when our agenda slot is over, we can self-organize to extend it into another agenda slot, making sure we post it on the wall for others to know, and/or find ways to continue the work on the issue beyond the conference.

One Law

The "law of two feet" encourages people to take responsibility for their own learning, peace of mind, and contribution. If someone is in a place where they feel they are not learning or able to contribute, the law of two feet encourages them to leave and move on to another group, where they think they might add more value, and feel more engaged. They may also choose to do something else altogether. Most importantly people shouldn't be somewhere where they feel they are wasting their time. From this law follows that some participants will become "bumblebees", people who fly from one session to another, and just like bees, cross-pollinate what is going on between sessions, and/or "butterflies", who choose at times to skip formal sessions and listen to their own sense of what they need to do in a given moment. Sometimes two butterflies meet outside of the sessions in informal conversation, and a new topic might arise out of that

> 'I can't imagine that there could be a better method for enabling a group to discover its potential.'
>
> Open Space practitioner

conversation. These principles and the law provide the *container* for the Open Space, enabling people to take full responsibility for their own learning and contribution. They create a context in which people can be focused and work hard, but remain flexible and open to surprise. "Be prepared to be surprised' is a typical reminder in an Open Space gathering.

With these basic instructions, the group is now ready to fill their empty wall (see following example). The facilitator asks people to think about their idea or burning question in response to the theme. After a short period of silence she invites whoever is ready to come to the centre, grab a marker and piece of paper, and write down their idea or question, read it out loud, and post it on the wall – choosing one of several pre-arranged space/time choices. Sometimes there are a few moments of quiet, but invariably people step up and begin to write and post sessions. Within a short period of time, the agenda for the day or for the week is laid out. People go up to the wall to read the different offerings, signing up for the groups they wish to join.

	Main Room	Tea Room	Lounge	Library	Garden
8:30-9:30	Community Meeting				
9:30-11:00					
11:30-13:00					
13:00-14:00	Lunch				
14:00-15:30					
16:00-17:30					
17:30-18:00	Convergence				

Now the work can begin. During a longer Open Space, the group will come back together as a whole for a brief meeting in the morning and evening, to report on main breakthroughs, to post new sessions as they occur to people, and to help maintain a sense of the whole. The facilitator of each group needs to compile the report of their session. Typically the outputs are typed and compiled during the duration of a meeting for people to go home with the final report.

Where decisions need to be made, time needs to be allowed for focusing and prioritizing the full output. This can be done in a matter of a few hours, even with larger groups.

Application

Open Space is being applied around the world. It has been used in townships in South Africa, in dialogues between Israelis and Palestinians in the Middle East, in many corporations, in the NGO sector for planning and community involvement, and in the Public Sector with similar uses. It can be used with 5 people or 1000. According to Harrison Owen, Open Space works best where conflict is present, things are complex, there is a huge diversity of players and the answer was needed yesterday. The personal investment is critical coupled with a real sense of urgency among participants. The greater the diversity, the higher the potential for real breakthrough and innovative outcomes. It works particularly well in the move from planning to action, where real action is facilitated by people stepping in and taking responsibility where they care.

Open Space can be run on its own, but it works equally well and sometimes better when combined with other tools and processes, such as World Café, Appreciative Inquiry, Scenario Planning, and others. In this case, using Open Space towards the end of a gathering is most typically the norm, allowing an initial process of clarifying ideas and views to be followed by stepping into taking responsibility for certain pieces.

Two Case Examples

The first case is a description taken from an article by Harrison Owen on the beginning of Open Space Technology. In the early summer of

1992, OST was used in one of the South African townships to promote useful discussion among several political groups. The focus of the conversation was on improving communications in the area. For a full day,

'The 2 days of Open Space that followed were a success, a miracle in the words of the CEO and he added that 3 years ago they received a thick report from a famous international strategic company meeting in Israel that cost $1.5 million, and they could hardly implement. Now we produced something much better in the cost of 1 page of their report, and it seems that we can implement it all.'

Avner Haramati

representatives of the various political parties along with nearby industry (largely white) worked together. It would be a supreme overstatement to say that all issues were resolved, or that love and light broke out in full abundance. But the discussions were intense, productive, without rancor, and contrasted sharply with conditions in a neighboring township where conversations had ceased and bloodshed commenced. There was also a continuing benefit. Several days after this particular gathering, one of the participants called to say that for two years as president of a local school organization, he had been attempting to get the people involved in creating their future. Nothing had worked. They sat like bumps on a log. Then he tried Open Space Technology, and his problem was reversed. The people became involved, and he had but one option, to get out of the way.

A second case shows an example of how Open Space together with an Appreciative Inquiry process helped an international organization build a common platform and plan for the future. Children's International Summer Villages (CISV) is a not-for-profit organization, which develops cross-cultural understanding in children and youth from around the world through peace education. They have over 60 national offices and wanted to develop a new strategic plan involving the grassroots of their organization. They decided to use an Appreciative Inquiry process with Open Space to combine the potential of Appreciative Inquiry to collect information, and build a shared foundation, direction and vision for the future with the potency of Open Space to mobilize people into action in areas they deeply care about.

Each country received a handbook explaining the Appreciative Inquiry process, and began a large-scale interview process to collect stories of personal experiences of inspiration and beauty that people carried with them from their time with the organization. Several thousand interviews were synthesized into a storybook with a summary of core values and wishes for the future.

The book became the foundation for a 2 1/2 day AI summit, in which people immersed themselves in the stories and data, building pride and clarity around what they do well and where they can naturally grow their strengths. From this, they developed tangible goals for the future (in the form of provocative propositions).

An overall umbrella theme for the future became the theme for a one day Open Space session, which included 150 people from across the world. The results were explosive. Lots of practical ideas, and plans, and focus areas emerged for CISV, which at the end were prioritized and voted on by the participants and several others who participated online. When reporting on outcomes from small groups, people related their reports to the overall goals, ensuring that everyone understood the implications of each report and how it tied to the overall vision before voting. Everyone, including online participants, voted on the top priorities for CISV. They also identified where they were willing to initiate moving the organization forward.

What they accomplished with this process was a plan, which had become alive in people and had in a sense begun even before the action steps were executed. They used AI and Open Space to rekindle grassroots passion, engaging commitment to implement from the outset.

Commentary

Open Space works particularly well when passion, engagement and burning questions Because Open Space is so versatile, we have given it a medium score on most of the categories of our method fingerprint. Of course, this is not to say that it is a mediocre tool. When used appropriately, it can make all the difference.

Open Space works particularly well when passion, engagement and burning questions are present. In such a situation, it truly helps a group move forward swiftly and clearly. On the other hand, it can fall flat when the engagement or interest is low. People need to be present because they want to be, not because they have been told they must be. For these reasons the intention is vital, as is expressing it clearly in the invitation to join an Open Space session, meeting or conference. With a clear intention and in the presence of a real need, Open Space is a beautiful testament to how little organizing is required by a planner when allowing people to self-organize their way forward. In fact, the art of the planner, with most potent Open Space sessions, is learning to truly get out of the way. This is also what makes Open Space a very accessible tool for new facilitators.

Purpose	Generating Awareness	✓✓
	Problem Solving	✓✓✓
	Building Relationships	✓✓
	Sharing Knowledge	✓✓✓
	Innovation	✓✓
	Shared Vision	✓✓
	Capacity Building	✓✓
	Pers./Leadersh. Dev.	✓✓
	Dealing with Conflict	✓✓
	Strat./Action Planning	✓✓✓
	Decision-Making	✓✓
Situation	Peaceful Situation	✓✓
	Conflictual Situation	✓
	High Complexity	✓✓
	Low Complexity	✓✓
Participants and Facilitation	Small Group (≤ 30)	✓✓
	Large Group (≥ 30)	✓✓
	Multi-Stakeholder	✓✓
	Peergroup	✓✓
	Div. of Power Levels	✓
	Div. Of Culture	✓✓
	Specific Facilitation Requirements	✓

Meanwhile, one of the reasons why it's often important to combine Open Space with other processes is that a key risk is that an Open Space conference ends without convergence happening among the different groups. A lot of great conversations may have happened in small groups, but they haven't been woven together adequately. Finding the ways to create this convergence and reconnection with the whole is an important challenge for facilitators and organizers using this process.

Also, while Harrison Owen points out that Open Space is useful in situations of conflict, in our experience the risk is that conflicting parties choose to just work with the people who agree with them. In that situation, combining it with processes that are more directly aimed at resolving conflict (rather than being productive in spite of conflict) can be useful. Similarly, while Open Space equalizes the *formal* power structures in that it gives individuals with less power an equal right to host sessions, other processes may be needed to work on the *informal* power dynamics in order to build the confidence and genuine freedom required for that to happen.

Open Space is all about handing the responsibility back to people themselves. Two core questions characterizing Open Space are: "What do you really want to do," and "why don't you take care of it?" As with the World Café and many other forms, the real art form lies in identifying the right calling question that truly draws people out of themselves and into a shared arena of thinking and acting together.

Resources

Owen, Harrison (1997). Expanding our now: The story of Open Space Technology.

Owen, Harrison (1997). Open Space Technology, A user's guide.

http://www.openspaceworld.com

Scenario Planning

Overview

Scenarios are possible and plausible pictures of the future. They are created through a series of conversations, in which a group of people invent and consider several varied stories about how the world may turn out in the future. Ideally, these stories should be carefully researched and full of detail, able to expose new understandings and some surprises. Scenarios are powerful tools for challenging current assumptions about the world, and in doing so, they lift the barriers of our own creativity and understanding about the future. The term "scenario planning" was originally coined by the RAND Corporation during and after World War II, as part of their corporate strategy. When Herman Kahn left the RAND Corporation, he set up the Hudson Institute and further developed the process, and went on to write a book called "The Year 2000" which was published in 1967. Since the late 60's, the process has taken off as a tool and has evolved considerably from its origins. Originally, scenario planning started with a paradigm of "predict and control", where probabilistic scenarios were sketched out about the future. This paradigm as a basis for the process has changed significantly over the years, mainly due to the work of Pierre Wack at Shell in the 1970's. Wack separated issues which were predictable from those which were uncertain, and worked with uncertainties and how they influenced various scenarios.

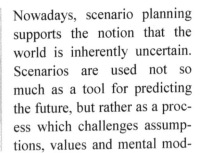

'Scenario-making is intensely participatory, or else it fails.'

Peter Schwartz

Nowadays, scenario planning supports the notion that the world is inherently uncertain. Scenarios are used not so much as a tool for predicting the future, but rather as a process which challenges assumptions, values and mental models of various stakeholders about how uncertainties might affect their collective futures. By encouraging scenario planning processes at different levels of an organization or community, old paradigms are challenged, and innovation encouraged through surprising possible stories of the future. Scenarios therefore help develop new and valuable knowledge.

By bringing multiple perspectives into a conversation about the future, a rich and multidimensional variety of scenarios are created. Scenarios encourage storytelling and dialogue among people who would not necessarily otherwise share their perspectives with each other.

Preparing for a Scenario Planning Process

Before embarking on a scenario process, it is important to establish whether it is the right process to use, and in what context it would be most useful. Scenarios are generally used when the following conditions exist:

- There is a high level of complexity in a given situation, which is difficult to understand

- There is a longer term (at least a few years ahead) focus required in looking into the future, and how to respond to it

- There is uncertainty about how the external environment will impact a particular situation

The scenario-planning process can then be adapted according to these specific questions:

- What is the purpose of this process?

- How many "players" need to be part of this process in order to view the necessary perspectives of the future?

- What parts of the external environment are important to focus on when considering these scenarios?

- Is there any level of control by any of the stakeholders of these external variables?

- What is the time horizon?

- Who is endorsing this process at a leadership level?

- Who needs to "buy-in" to the potential outcomes?

- There are resources available to invest in a series of conversations amongst different stakeholders over a period of time, and to distribute these scenarios extensively.

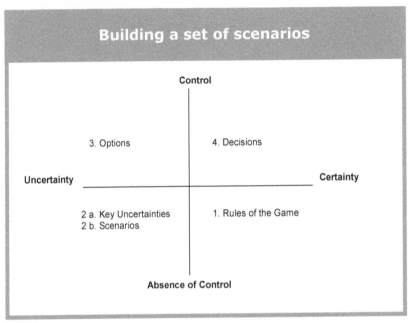

Scenarios can also be very broad and are not necessarily useful if the focus and purpose is unclear. Once a particular organization or community has decided to use scenarios, the following questions will help make the outcome relevant to all concerned.

The Process

There are many ways of developing scenarios. The process below is but one simple example of how to facilitate a scenario-building exercise, which considers the important principles of uncertainty and control. South Africans Chantal Illbury and Clem Sunter have mapped out this process for building a set of scenarios to consider for future strategy.

The horizontal axis represents the continuum of certainty/ uncertainty, and the vertical axis represents the continuum of control/ absence of control. All of the steps of this scenario process are numbered in order and move through the four quadrants highlighted in the diagram. The scenarios themselves are generally based on a set of different uncertainties which may play out in the future, and where there is absence of control by the "players" of the game. The steps of the process are explained as follows:

a. *What are the rules?*

In any given situation, rules of "the game" are certain, but not necessarily controllable. "The game" is a metaphor of the context being examined in the scenario process. It is important to firstly distinguish between the written and unwritten rules of the game. The unwritten rules can also be referred to as "tacit", and are often socially constructed. By surfacing these unwritten rules, it is easier to better understand "the game". On the other hand, written rules are often aspirational – they are aspired to by the organization, but not necessarily implemented in reality.

b. *What are the key uncertainties?*

The next step in this scenario process is to map out the key uncertainties for the future. This is a highly creative step, where it is important to get multiple perspectives of what is uncertain. By mapping the key uncertainties in order of importance and level of predictability, the group can start to decide which ones to explore in more detail to start developing scenarios. The diagram below assists the process of prioritizing scenarios:

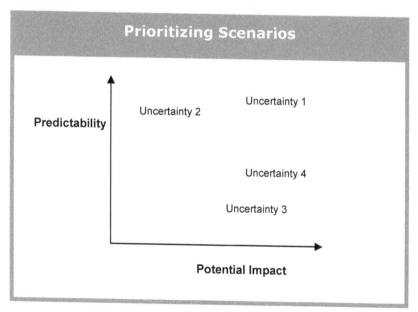

c. *Develop the scenarios*

As mentioned above, scenarios can be viewed as multiple pictures of the future. This glimpse can give participants an understanding of what is possible, and the motivation to plan towards their preferred scenario. A useful technique to decide on the preferred scenarios is to expand on the key uncertainties by examining the possible outcomes of those uncertainties. For example, in a country context, one of the uncertainties might be economic growth. So the scenarios could explore the stories which would unfold if there would be high economic growth or low economic growth. To give a scenario a more multi-dimensional aspect, two key uncertainties could be explored – see graph below. Scenarios are developed to surprise us, and to bring to the surface possibilities we wouldn't normally anticipate for the future. This means it is important to base the scenarios on uncertainties which have low predictability and high impact (uncertainties 3 and 4 in graph above). The graph below is an example of scenarios which are developed based on 2 key uncertainties.

d. *Identify options for future action*

Options are determined from the scenarios. The scenarios can be seen

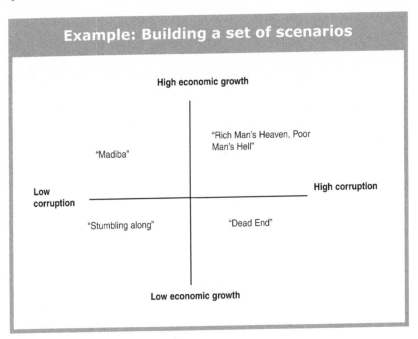

as the bridge between the key uncertainties and options – they help order a group process in a way that paints a set of vivid and detailed pictures of what is possible, and therefore the possibility to map out options to match each of these scenarios. It is therefore important that the scenarios are written up in a lot of detail, so that all components of a given situation are explored. This will assist the process of mapping out options of action for each scenario.

e. *Take decisions*

The final stage is to make decisions based on the scenarios and the options. The key question in this phase is: "If Scenario X will become reality one day, what should we do today in preparation?" Illbury & Sunter refer to George Kelley who introduces us to the "personal construct theory".

He claims that we make decisions based on our own interpretations of the world, which are informed by our experiences. If our experiences are cut off from those of others, we limit the quality of the decisions we make. Scenarios help bring these different experiences into pictures of the future through a dialogue, which in turn helps us make more informed decisions for the future.

Applications

Scenario Methods have been used since the 1960s. Back then, the process was mostly used within companies to help them make more informed long-term decisions. Since then, the process has been more widely applied to social contexts with multiple stakeholder involvement. Scenarios have been used extensively all over the world in varied contexts from mapping out country strategies (Jamaica, South Africa, Botswana, Kenya and others) to corporate strategies (Shell, Anglo American, OldMutual), as well as at multiple community levels.

Case Example: Mont Fleur Scenario-Process, South Africa

In his book, *Solving Tough Problems*, Adam Kahane tells the story of facilitating the Mont Fleur Scenarios. In 1991, 22 influential South African figures came together for a scenario-building process about the future of the country. It was shortly after Nelson Mandela's release, when the future of South Africa was very uncertain. The group attending included leaders from the left (African National Congress, Pan-African Congress, National Union of Mineworkers, South African Communist Party), as well as their adversaries from white business and academia. They all saw the reality of South Africa from different perspectives. The group sat for a couple of days talking to each other. They met multiple times over a period of months, and talked through a number of scenarios. They eventually decided on four scenarios they found most plausible for South Africa. These scenarios were all based on the question of: "How will the transition go, and will the country succeed in "taking off"?

The four stories were based on bird analogies. Firstly, there was the Ostrich, where the white government sticks its head in the sand to avoid a negotiated settlement. Then there was the Lame Duck where the transition goes on for too long, trying to satisfy all parties and not succeeding. Thirdly, there was Icarus, where a black government comes to power and institutes a massive public spending policy which bankrupts the economy. Finally, the most positive scenario was The Flight of the Flamingos, where a successful transition takes place, and everyone in South Africa slowly rises together. From the group, the Flamingo scenario was unanimously agreed on as the best alternative. These scenarios were written up in a rich 25-page report and distributed widely through the media and workshops all over the country. From these multiple engagements, the outcomes of Mont Fleur had a significant effect on the economic policy of South Africa. Many leaders and politicians have referred to these scenarios in various debates and discussions.

This process was so remarkably successful for four overarching reasons:

- The timing was right – it was the window of opportunity to create a new future at the beginning of South Africa's transition. There was much uncertainty and absence of control.

- There was top political buy-in and participation at all levels.

- The process itself built meaningful relationships, and all involved bought into the scenarios.

- The follow-up was extensive – the stories were well written in detail, and communicated through mass media, television, and workshops. Many political speeches and strategy sessions referred to this documentation.

These scenarios proved to be powerful tools for both planning and debate, and are still spoken of over 10 years later. The Mont Fleur process highlights the impact of facilitated dialogue about the future, and the power of stories.

Commentary

Many organizations work in an increasingly complex situation both internally and externally. When we are faced with complex systems, one of the key capacities that is needed is to be able to not only work from one point of view or frame of reference, but from many. Scenarios help us to work simultaneously with more than one perspective and story, and to take actions that make sense across multiple frames. The real power of the scenario planning process is the ability to bring many different stakeholders into a conversation about the future, creating collective ownership of a set of pictures, and building important relationships across differences.

Purpose	Generating Awareness	✓✓
	Problem Solving	✓✓
	Building Relationships	✓✓
	Sharing Knowledge	✓✓
	Innovation	✓✓✓
	Shared Vision	✓✓✓
	Capacity Building	✓
	Pers./Leadersh. Dev.	✓✓
	Dealing with Conflict	✓
	Strat./Action Planning	✓✓✓
	Decision-Making	✓✓
Situation	Peaceful Situation	✓✓
	Conflictual Situation	✓
	High Complexity	✓✓✓
	Low Complexity	✓
Participants and Facilitation	Small Group (≤ 30)	✓✓
	Large Group (≥ 30)	✓✓
	Multi-Stakeholder	✓✓✓
	Peergroup	✓
	Div. of Power Levels	✓✓
	Div. Of Culture	✓✓
	Specific Facilitation Requirements	✓✓

The outcome of a scenario-building process can be useful in two ways:

- *Firstly*, the set of possible stories of the future helps a group/ organization/ community to respond in a timely fashion should a crisis arise. This is a more reactive approach to scenario work, in that the scenarios chosen at the end may not have an order of preference (good or bad, desirable or undesirable), but are simply mapping out implications of various possible "futures". The primary purpose of this outcome would be to respond in a more informed manner to situations before they arise.

- *Secondly*, a more proactive response would be to strive towards the scenario of choice, and map out strategies to help a group move towards that picture. Scenarios would therefore have an order of preference amongst stakeholders involved, and the most preferred scenario is the one to strive for. Peter Drucker once said: "The best way to predict the future is to create it". Scenarios are a powerful way of moving towards a more desired future, as has been highlighted by the outcome of the Mont Fleur scenarios. The process and examples we have used in this explanation demonstrates this view of futurist thinking.

Resources

Hansen, M. et al. (1999). What's Your Strategy for Managing Knowledge? In Harvard Business Review: 106-117

Illbury, C & **Sunter, C**. (2001). The Mind of a Fox: Scenario Planning in Action.

Schwartz, P. (1991). The Art of the Long View: Planning for an Uncertain World.

Van der Heijden, K. (1996). The Art of Strategic Conversation.

Kahane, A. (2004). Solving Tough Problems.

Senge, P. et al. (1994). The 5th Discipline Fieldbook.

Sustained Dialogue

Overview

The key distinguishing feature of Sustained Dialogue is precisely that it is sustained. Over extended periods of time, the same group of people join in consecutive meetings. The underlying assumption behind this is that, in order to address conflictual issues, we need to look beyond the concrete problem to be solved, and focus on the underlying relationships of the issue. Moreover, changing relationships is a dynamic, non-linear process which takes time and requires commitment from those involved. It doesn't happen in a day or at a brief workshop. Sustained Dialogue was developed primarily by veteran US diplomat Dr. Harold Saunders, who was inspired by a long career in international affairs and peace processes. Key to the inspiration behind Sustained Dialogue was his work as co-chair of the "Dartmouth Conferences", an unofficial, multilevel, unique peace-making venture between the US and the USSR, started in 1960 and continued over a process of more than 30 years.

Over years, the same participants sustained their conversation from one meeting to the next, speaking with an increasing sense of freedom, reaching greater and greater depth, and building trusting relationships and a foundation of shared knowledge. The agenda was open-ended and cumulative, allowing participants to pick out themes and take them to their logical conclusion, and allowing new themes to arise.

In 1992, members of the Dartmouth Conference's Regional Conflicts Task Force decided to draw on their experience to foster dialogue in a national conflict in Tajikistan, and it was through this work that Sustained Dialogue was further elaborated and conceptualized into its current basic model.

While the process was born from situations of conflict and extreme stress, it reflects a universal pattern of human relationships, and can be used in a variety of community, corporate, regional and national settings. This section is based on writings of Harold Saunders as well as an interview and materials provided by Teddy Nemeroff, while he was working with the Institute for Democracy in South Africa (IDASA) specifically on Sustained Dialogue. Nemeroff has worked with Sustained Dialogue in a wider range of contexts beyond the international peace-building arena, including on youth issues, local governance, and with universities. He launched the Sustained Dialogue program at Princeton University, which since evolved into a program at 10 US university campuses, specifically looking at race relations among students.

Sustained Dialogue is informed by two conceptual frameworks: five elements of relationships and five stages of a sustained dialogue.

The Five Elements of Relationships

As mentioned above, the focus of Sustained Dialogue is on the underlying relationships that affect a given problem. Given this focus, it is important to understand what is meant by relationships and what the different aspects of relationship are. The following five components or arenas of interaction make up a definition of relationships. They work in constantly changing combinations.

- *Identity*: The way that participants define themselves including the life experiences they bring to the present moment
- *Interests*: The things people care about, that are drawing them together
- *Power*: The capacity to influence a course of events
- *Perceptions of the Other*: Including misperceptions and stereotypes
- *Patterns of Interaction*: Including respect for certain limits on behavior

This framework is analytical but also operational in the sense that participants in a Sustained Dialogue will usually be introduced to these elements and will draw on them in understanding the nature of the relationships that divide them. Sometimes participants can find it hard to talk about relationships, but they become apparent in the dialogues to both participants and moderators. In that situation, this framework provides a point of reference.

The Five Stages of Sustained Dialogue

The Sustained Dialogue process is mapped out in five stages. These stages have been identified, not based on what the creators of the process necessarily would want to happen, but rather on what they observed happening as a natural evolution when participants came together in a dialogue sustained over time. It is important to point out that these stages are a kind of ideal description and not a recipe. Generally participants will move back and forth between the stages, and will not follow them rigidly. Also, the Sustained Dialogue facilitator will not push them through the process although this basic pattern provides a sense of direction for both participants and facilitators to a process that is otherwise open-ended.

> 'I would as a white student talk about interacting with a black student, and how it was uncomfortable. A black student would tell a story about how a white student treated them. Stage Three would be where someone would say 'maybe our experience is similar'. 'Maybe in my story, the way I felt is like how the white person in your story felt.' This is where we are getting into each other's shoes.'
>
> Teddy Nemeroff (Interview)

Stage One - *Deciding to Engage*

First a group of participants needs to be convened. A good size for a Sustained Dialogue is 8-12 people. They should ideally be people who are respected community leaders (but not necessarily in official positions), who reflect the key viewpoints of the topic, conflict, or community, and who are willing to come together to listen to one another in an ongoing process. Though Sustained Dialogue is intended and designed to shift relationships, the participants will generally be coming together because they are motivated by, and focused on, a particular problem. They don't necessarily see relationships as the heart of that problem from the outset.

Convening an appropriate group of participants can be a difficult and drawn out process. It may be hard to get them to commit the time, to accept the value of the process, or to be willing to engage with others where there is a dysfunctional relationship. Their motivation to join will depend on whether they are the right people to be involved, whether they have a compelling desire to solve a problem, whether they are aware of their common interest and interdependence in solving it, and whether the conveners succeed in communicating the value of the dialogue process.

Once the participants have been identified, Stage One is also the time where they together agree on the purpose, scope, and ground rules of the dialogue. Sometimes the participants actually sign a "covenant" to contract with each other.

Stage Two - *Mapping Relationships and Naming Problems*

This is where the conversations actually begin. Stage Two is first a process of naming the issues – telling stories of personal experiences, venting grievances, downloading or "dumping" all the concerns, letting it all out, and clearing the air. Towards the later parts of this stage, participants will start to map the problems and the related underlying relationships out in a more structured way and they will identify a few major issues they want to focus on in a deeper exploration.

Stage Three: *Probing Problems and Relationships*

At the end of Stage Two and beginning of Stage 3, the character of the conversation shifts. "Me" becomes "We". "What" becomes "Why". Participants shift from speaking "to" each other to speaking "with" each other. The group is finding patterns and explanations, making connections, and developing concepts. They are more interpretive and analytical at this stage, probing the dynamics of the underlying relationships causing their problems, and identifying broad possible ways into changing those relationships. The group is now focusing on some narrower or deeper issues or leverage points in the system, bearing in mind the connections to the other issues that were mapped in Stage Two. They are arriving at the insights that will drive their choices for action. They are also accessing their individual and collective will to enact change, and coming to a sense of direction.

Stage Four: *Scenario-building*

While the group has been primarily focused on problems until this point, they now step into a positive solution space. They work out what practical steps need to be taken in order to change troublesome relationships and to overcome obstacles. If the dialogue is related to the political level, they will suggest steps to be taken in the political arena, and they may relate to actions to be taken by influential players beyond the dialogue group. If it is at a more local or organizational level, the dialogue group may be focusing more on designing its own direct actions. These may be collective or individual.

The use of the word "scenarios" to describe this stage in Sustained Dialogue is quite different from its use in our above description of scenario-planning. A Sustained Dialogue facilitator could choose to do an actual scenario-planning process in this stage, but the stage is really about defining scenarios in the very broad sense of simply sketching options for action and possible ways forward.

Stage Five: *Acting Together*

In Stage Five the shift is from talking to action and the previously inwardly directed focus is redirected outward. The participants are now either working out how to put their suggestions into the hands of those who can implement them, or they figure out how to implement the necessary activities themselves. The nature of this action depends greatly on the subject of the dialogue, the level of influence of members, the level of risk involved, and the specific context in which it is taking place. This may either be the conclusion of the process, or it may be the start of addressing a new, probably previously raised, issue.

As stated earlier, these five stages are not linear, but there are some patterns even in their non-linearity: a genuine and effective Stage Three will typically depend on the group having gone through Stage Two, so it would generally not happen that a group skips from Stage One to Three. They may oscillate back and forth quite a bit between Two and Three though, and then jump to Stage Four when ready.

In Stages Three-Five especially the difference between the diplomatic/political level work with Sustained Dialogue and the more community/youth level work is apparent. There is a lot of diversity in how these stages play out in different processes, and Sustained Dialogue takes a healthy open-ended approach to that variety. As the group moves through the five stages, they will usually increasingly take ownership of the process and sometimes completely self-manage it. It is important to have a facilitator guiding them through it, who understands the needs of the group and who is able to recognize the five stages and help the transitions to happen without pushing the group into a new stage prematurely. The style of facilitation and the degree to which the facilitator intervenes will vary greatly from dialogue to dialogue. At times, the facilitator may not need to say anything at all. Other times, s/he may be intervening much more directly, in a more workshop-style form. This depends on the characteristics of the dialogue group and what elements of the relationships present emerge at any given time.

Applications

Sustained Dialogue is being applied in several distinct types of settings. Hal Saunders and the Kettering Institute focus on its effectiveness in conflict resolution at a political or social level. In addition to the extensive work in Tajikistan they have applied it in Azerbaijan/Armenia/Nagorno-Karabakh, in the Middle East and other places. As mentioned above, Teddy Nemoroff's work at Princeton has led it to being used on about 10 university campuses in the US, primarily focusing on improving race relations. The below case is from the work that Nemeroff did with IDASA (the Institute for Democracy in South Africa) in South Africa and Zimbabwe.

Case Example-IDASA Youth Project in Zimbabwe

In a time of deepening crisis in Zimbabwe, youth are a particularly vulnerable group. They run an increased risk of contracting HIV/AIDS and suffer greatly under the economic collapse and high unemployment. These factors contribute to a situation where youth are being taken advantage of by political parties. From May 2004 through December 2005, IDASA supported a Sustained Dialogue initiative to empower youth in Zimbabwe in collaboration with the Coordinating Committee of the Organizations for Voluntary Service (COSV), and its Zimbabwean partner the Amani Trust. The intention of this project was to reduce the political exploitation of youth and to strengthen their self-reliance by building relationships, developing a deeper understanding of their issues of concern, and developing actions to improve their lives. The project engaged 120 youth leaders in Harare from across the socio-economic and political spectrum.

The collaboration among the Zimbabwean organizations originally was formed as a media and advocacy campaign, mobilizing 14 Zimbabwean NGOs to participate. But as this became an increasingly risky political exercise, they decided to try Sustained Dialogue instead. This shift significantly changed the scale of the project, now reaching only about 120 rather than the intended 1000's. But depth of impact replaced breadth. The project worked strategically with youth leaders who could subsequently make a positive difference in their communities, and this impact could be more easily monitored. Also, rather than the message being defined centrally and broadcast to the youth, the youth defined the issues they wanted to focus on themselves, primarily unemployment and HIV/AIDS.

Eight youth dialogue groups of 15 members each were launched simultaneously throughout the capital city of Harare. Each had one youth and one NGO activist as co-moderators, who were trained in Sustained Dialogue by IDASA. These moderators held orientation sessions for the participants, where expectations were aligned and discussion topics were selected. The groups launched at two-day overnight retreats, after which they started meeting at monthly half-day meetings at venues in their communities. The groups started out cautiously because of the political situation and the sensitivity of the issue of HIV/AIDS, but as they progressed and trust increased, they began opening up and sharing more intimately.

The political climate and events in Zimbabwe made it difficult for the project to function and for youth to reach the meeting places. Despite these challenges, the project achieved significant results. It succeeded in creating spaces for talking and thinking together about their challenges. Half of the groups managed to engage youth from both sides of the political spectrum while all of them managed to bring in a diversity of interests and backgrounds. The participants gained knowledge about

Purpose	Generating Awareness	✓✓✓
	Problem Solving	✓✓
	Building Relationships	✓✓✓
	Sharing Knowledge	✓✓✓
	Innovation	✓
	Shared Vision	✓✓
	Capacity Building	✓
	Pers./Leadersh. Dev.	✓✓
	Dealing with Conflict	✓✓
	Strat./Action Planning	✓✓
	Decision-Making	✓
Situation	Peaceful Situation	✓
	Conflictual Situation	✓✓
	High Complexity	✓✓
	Low Complexity	✓
Participants and Facilitation	Small Group (≤ 30)	✓✓✓
	Large Group (≥ 30)	✓
	Multi-Stakeholder	✓✓
	Peergroup	✓✓
	Div. of Power Levels	✓✓
	Div. Of Culture	✓✓
	Specific Facilitation Requirements	✓✓

the issues, an increased sense of agency, stronger relationships and skills in dialogue and conflict management. This led to increased youth leadership in the communities, mitigation of community conflicts, and youth violence, and the development of plans for addressing community challenges.

Commentary

According to Nemeroff, there are two questions to be asked. The first is: Will dialogue and improved relationships help this situation and is it worth the effort? Convening and sustaining a Sustained Dialogue can be a lot of work. The second question is: Is the timing right and how is this going to interact with the context, with what is going on in the outside world? Will it conflict with other processes that are already going on to try and resolve the issue? Sustained Dialogue is most useful in situations where relationships are dysfunctional, where there is a lack of trust, and official processes are not working because the issues are not easily solved in a negotiation-type setup. Sustained Dialogue is not a space for debate or for official negotiations among formal representatives. It is also not a purely interpersonal process, nor is it a skills training. And it is certainly not a quick fix. The strength of Sustained Dialogue is in its flexibility and simplicity. The open-endedness allows a group to go where it needs to go, and it is important to look not only for the expected impact, but also for the positive unexpected results.

The main challenge is that it isn't a ready-made methodology, with a step-by-step guide. The two frameworks – the five elements of relationship and the five stages of Sustained Dialogue – provide a very basic but useful sense of direction and reference point. This means that the process relies greatly on the intuition of the facilitator, as well as his/her skills, personal attitudes and capacities, and contextual understanding. The facilitator needs to be able to respond to a wide variety of situations and to draw on a wide repertoire of possible ways of interacting in the group. Besides the nature of this process as being sustained over time, another aspect that strikes us about this process as distinguishing it from most of the others in this collection is the nature of Stage Two and the transition to Stage Three. To us, venting seems to be highly underrated in many processes. The release participants get from letting everything out and getting things off their chest, and the shift that happens when this has been done, can be highly generative.

Resources

Saunders, Harold A. (1999). Public Peace Process: Sustained Dialogue to Transform Racial and Ethnic Conflicts

Sustained Dialogue: A Citizen's Peace Building Process – Guide prepared by **Teddy Nemoroff**

Diving In: A Handbook for Improving Race Relations on College Campuses Through the Process of Sustained Dialogue By **Teddy Nemeroff** & **David Tukey**

Empowering Zimbabwean Youth Through Sustained Dialogue by **Teddy Nemeroff** (case study prepared for UNDP)

www.sdcampusnetwork.org

www.sustaineddialogue.org

www.kettering.org

The World Café

Overview

The World Café is an intentional way to create a living network of conversations around questions that matter. It is a methodology which enables (12 to 1200!) people to think together and intentionally create new, shared meaning and collective insight. Although people have been meeting in ways sharing the same spirit of the World Café for centuries, the actual methodology was 'discovered' and formalized by Juanita Brown and David Isaacs in 1995. Since then, hundreds of thousands of people have been meeting in World Café style across the world.

The host of a World Café makes use of the café metaphor quite literally. The room is actually set up like a café, with people sitting in groups of four at different tables, for deeply participative, high-quality conversations. They are guided to move to new tables as part of a series of conversational rounds around questions that matter to them. With each move, a table host remains behind, sharing the essence of his/her table's conversation. The others move out into the room and connect to what other tables have talked about, in this way networking and cross-pollinating the conversations. The café format, with its ability to weave and further build insights, new ideas or new questions, enables collective intelligence to evolve within a group.

The World Café is based on a core assumption that the knowledge and wisdom that we need is already present and accessible. Working with the World Café, we can bring out the collective wisdom of the group - greater than the sum of its individual parts - and channel it towards positive change. Finn Voldtofte, one of the early World Café pioneers actually sees the café as the unit of change force in any system or organization as it engages, inspires and connects different parts of a system.

As Margaret Mead once said: *Never doubt that small groups of committed people can change the world. Indeed it is the only thing that ever has.*

Four conditions to create café magic

Many people, who have participated in a really energetic and effective World Café, speak of the human "magic" that arose in the conversations and exchanges, as they moved from one to another conversation, evolving a theme or deepening a question. Through the work of café practitioners, four conditions have been identified that enable 'café magic' to occur:

1. *A question that matters*: Identifying compelling questions is an art form. For a question to matter to a group, it needs to have personal relevance to each person. They need to be invested with a real stake in the question and its answers. Good questions open up to a diverse range of thinking, are thought provoking and stimulate creativity. A good question places the ball in the court of the participants – showing them they are needed, valuable contributors to the whole.

2. *A safe and hospitable space*: Often meeting spaces are not very inviting. Here the café metaphor gets played out, and care is taken to create an inviting and warm environment. Usually it is complete with café tables, table-cloths, flowers and candles. When people step into the World Café, they immediately know that this is not just another formal meeting. In addition to the physical environment, though, is the creation of an actually safe space, where people feel comfortable enough to contribute what they are thinking and feeling. If for example a group from the same organization participates in a World Café, care should be taken that people know they will not be punished later for saying something in disagreement with a colleague or superior.

3. *Mutual listening*: This condition emphasizes the importance of listening over talking. It connects to the underlying assumption that the knowledge and wisdom we need is already present. Collective insight will only emerge as we honor and encourage each person's unique contribution. Margaret Wheatley has said that *Intelligence emerges as a system connects with itself in new and diverse ways*. As each person offers his or her perspective, they are contributing to the increasing intelligence and insight of the whole, often in surprising ways.

4. *A spirit of inquiry*: In the World Café, a spirit of inquiry is key. This means that people are truly in exploration together. They bring what they know, think and feel about a given question to the table, but they are willing to go beyond that, to work together to uncover new insights, different perspective, and deeper questions. We can all always learn more. Fostering a spirit of inquiry and curiosity for what is not known, will help overcome resistance to new or different thoughts.

The World Café homepage suggests that a simple way to invite participants to engage optimally in the World Café is by sharing the following "Café Etiquette" with them:

- Focus on what matters

- Contribute your thinking and experience

- Speak from the heart

- Listen to understand

- Link and connect ideas

- Listen together for deeper themes, insights and questions.

- Play, Doodle, Draw—writing on the tablecloths is encouraged!

The following guidelines are directly related to the four conditions, and can help a facilitator to enable the creation of these conditions.

- Clarify the purpose: Before bringing together people for a café, clarify the purpose of the café. Understanding the purpose is necessary to be able to decide who should be there, the questions to discuss and the finer details of the design.

- Create Hospitable Space

- Explore Questions that Matter: Don't underestimate the care needed to succeed in identifying good questions.

- Encourage Each Person's Contribution

- Connect Diverse People and Ideas: The opportunity to move between tables, meet new people, actively contribute your thinking, and link discoveries is one of the distinguishing characteristics of the World Café. Design your cafe for maximum cross-pollinating without making the rounds themselves too short.

- Listen for Insights and Share Discoveries: Encourage each café group to take a bit of time for reflection to notice *what's at the center of our conversation?* After several rounds of café conversation it is helpful to engage in a conversation of the whole group to explore together which themes and questions are arising.

Applications

The World Café website and the new book released in 2005 about the World Café profile numerous stories of how this approach has been used in different contexts across cultures, sectors, social classes, and generations. According to the website, the World Café is valuable when you aim:

- to generate input, share knowledge, stimulate innovative thinking, and explore action possibilities around real life issues and questions

- To engage people - whether they are meeting for the first time, or are in established relationships - in authentic conversation

- To conduct in-depth exploration of key strategic challenges or opportunities

- To deepen relationships and mutual ownership of outcomes in an existing group

- To create meaningful interaction between a speaker and the audience

- To engage groups larger than 12 (up to 1200!) in an authentic dialogue process

The café is less useful if there is a predetermined outcome, there is a desire to convey one-way information, or a group is working on detailed implementation plans.

Case Examples – From Maori Forestry Claims to Norwegian Town Planning

The café is a simple but efficient tool, which has been used in many different settings. We include three examples to show its breadth of use. These cases have been chosen from the World Café website www.theworldcafé.com.

- In New Zealand the Café was used by an organization to create a gathering to increase knowledge, networking and agreement among diverse Maori groups all working to claim back forests from the Ministry of Justice. The informal warm atmosphere of the World Café worked incredibly well with the traditional ways of the indigenous Maori people.

  Experts on the claims process were brought in to provide insights and perspective, and conversations among claimant groups and others around tables occurred throughout. The purpose was to progress Maori treaty claims, and the process was to hear diverse views, network with those who knew more, and to consider next steps. This first three day café looks likely to spark several others in other regions in New Zealand, with an intention that the final outcome is a vision of partnership between the Maori and non-Maori people of the land.

- The World Café has also proven itself as a tool for town planning in Norway. The head of culture for a suburb of Oslo made use of the café as a way to get input and involvement from citizens involved in culture for a plan for the cultural activities of the future. They were used to people being rather passive at town meetings, and so the World Café was brought in as a way to fully engage people. The café kicked off with a simple exercise that everyone had to join in: The participants had to draw a simple picture to express what they wanted to achieve with culture in their community. From here, they began sharing their ideas, writing down comments, insights and questions on the tablecloth. Weaving in and out between groups, they gathered new ideas or solutions to elaborate on. Each table had members of the cultural department helping to gather the main ideas that would later be used in the formal cultural plan. The set-up and structure of the café meant that everyone became deeply involved in thinking together around the issues, challenges and possibilities of culture in the future of the town. Ideas that could work for many sectors had been shared. The informal creation of relations and the creation of a sense of wholeness in the group was a very important side-benefit. At the end of the meeting, the main learning for the organizers was that it is much more important to find ways to engage the energy and commitment of the people who are involved, than it is to produce a piece of paper with the formal plan.

- Our third example is the Financial Planning Association – a membership association of financial planners in the US. They have been making use of café as a way to build their new organization after a merger of two independent groups. During the first year, they hosted around 15 cafes, described as falling into three overarching categories:

Member cafes were cafés for members that mostly focused on bringing members together for networking. The questions asked were very broad and simply aimed to generate stimulating conversation and new insights together.

Event-driven cafes were cafes integrated as part of existing events for the different constituencies of the association. These enabled people to participate in technically specific conversations, learning from each other in the process. The goals of most of these were personal and business specific notes that the participants took for themselves.

Purpose driven cafes were convened with a very specific purpose in mind and some kind of expected outcome, such as reaching consensus on a major decision, or planning specific workgroup activities.

Commentary

The World Café is a strong tool to ignite and engage a large group of people through meaningful questions and an inviting, safe space. The process of bringing diverse perspectives and ideas together can give a group a sense of their collective intelligence and wisdom that is larger than the sum of the parts. The World Café can be used within as little as an hour, or be convened as a gathering over several days. As a standalone tool, the Café is stronger in opening up possibilities than in converging around plans or decisions, and so if it is part of a longer gathering it is often used in combination with other tools. For example, the divergence and breadth of ideas generated through a Café could be followed up with an Open Space process, in which participants have to step in and take responsibility for specific areas or issues. Meanwhile, the Café can also offer a useful alternative to more formal approaches to reporting back from small groups like task-forces, committees, or Open Space groups. Rather than having each group stand in front of a plenary to speak to words on a flipchart, a Café can be created where people from different groups move between the tables and capture the key insights.

Purpose	Generating Awareness	✓✓
	Problem Solving	✓✓✓
	Building Relationships	✓✓✓
	Sharing Knowledge	✓✓✓
	Innovation	✓✓
	Shared Vision	✓✓
	Capacity Building	✓✓
	Pers./Leadersh. Dev.	✓✓
	Dealing with Conflict	✓
	Strat./Action Planning	✓
	Decision-Making	✓
Situation	Peaceful Situation	✓✓
	Conflictual Situation	✓✓
	High Complexity	✓✓
	Low Complexity	✓✓
Participants and Facilitation	Small Group (≤ 30)	✓✓
	Large Group (≥ 30)	✓✓✓
	Multi-Stakeholder	✓✓
	Peergroup	✓✓
	Div. of Power Levels	✓✓✓
	Div. Of Culture	✓✓✓
	Specific Facilitation Requirements	✓

The World Café can be great for equalizing power because people sit in diverse groups at small tables. A CEO and an intern, or a UN official and a streetkid, may sit together, and the tables are so small that everyone generally must participate. Sometimes it may be important to give instructions about who people need to sit with, or to put marks at the tables symbolizing different types of participants, so they can deliberately sit together. It can be important when planning a café where the participant group will be characterized by diversity of power, to make sure that people know what they are getting into, as it may otherwise meet resistance from those of higher rank. A skilled facilitator will know though how to incorporate such tension as learning for the group. Meaningful questions are absolutely essential for a successful Café. However, questions that may matter to the organizers may not be as compelling for the participants. Where a designer of a World Café process is not sure of the questions that will ignite the passions of a group, he or she can simply ask an initial question which seeds further questions, eg. What question, if answered, would make the greatest difference to the future of the situation we're exploring here?

Resources

Brown, Juanita and **David Isaacs** (2005). The World Café: Shaping Our Futures through Conversations that Matter

http://www.theworldcafe.com

Additional Tools

The universe of Dialogue Methodologies seems to be infinite. In addition to the ten tools we covered in depth, we have, through experience and research, come across a wide variety of other approaches. In this section, we briefly portray some of these additional tools – they simply deserve to be mentioned.

Bohmian Dialogue

'What is the source of all this trouble? I'm saying that the source is basically in thought. Many people would think that such a statement is crazy; because thought is the one thing we have with which to solve our problems. That's part of our tradition. Yet it looks as if the thing we use to solve our problems with is the source of our problems. It's like going to the doctor and having him make you ill. In fact, in 20% of medical cases we do apparently have that going on. But in the case of thought, its far over 20%.' – David Bohm

The famous quantum physicist David Bohm (1917-1992) made many significant contributions to theoretical physics, particularly in quantum mechanics and relativity theory. At the same time, Bohm is one of the most quoted people in the field of dialogue theory und methods. The connection from physics to dialogue may at first seem unclear. However, Bohm's understanding of physics was deeply aligned with his view of the nature of reality, the nature of thought and the meaning of dialogue, and the connections among them. Throughout his life, he was actively involved in politics and philosophy, with one of his key inspirations being the Indian philosopher J. Krishnamurti.

We include David Bohm's approach to dialogue in this collection because it is a unique method in its own right. However, it's important to recognize that the Bohmian dialogue is far more than a method. It's a philosophy and a worldview, which we can only introduce very briefly here. Bohm believed that thought shapes our reality, and that dialogue shapes thought and thought processes in turn. He used to emphasize that dialogue comes from the roots *dia* (through) and *logos* (meaning) and so to him the word *dialogue* signified *meaning flowing through us*. He saw dialogue as a process of direct face-to-face encounter by which people could participate in a common pool of meaning – a kind of "shared mind" or "collective intelligence". It was not a process by which one person would try to convince everyone else of his/her idea, but rather where the participants would engage in creating a common understanding. To him, thought was one big process, and it didn't really make sense to break it up into *my thought* and *your thought*.

'Dialogue is really aimed at going into the whole thought process and changing the way the thought process occurs collectively. We haven't really paid much attention to thought as a process. We have engaged in thoughts, but we have only paid attention to the content, not to the process.'

David Bohm

To many of the global crises Bohm observed, he attributed patterns of fragmentation in life, communication and society. Bohm stipulated a breakdown in communication and relationships, and he believed that the key problem was an incoherence of thought, and an inability to see how our own thinking behaves, and how the process of thought creates even more problems than it solves. The overriding intention with his approach to dialogue was to understand consciousness, to explore day-to-day relationships and communication, and to overcome fragmentation.

In a Bohmian dialogue, 15-40 people convene in a circle. This range of group size is specified as a number that is not too large for depth and intimacy but large enough to allow subcultures to form and become visible. The groups generally meet more than once, for about two hours at a time, regularly over an extended period of time.

There is no pre-set agenda. The idea is that the absence of an agenda allows for meaning to flow freely and undirected. The group decides when they meet what they would like to talk about and how they would like to proceed. It is important to emphasize here that the fact that there is no objective or intended outcome for the dialogue, does not mean there is no reason for it. As the group stays with the process over time, the deeper meanings are revealed. The dialogue leads to increased coherence, creativity, and fellowship.

This process of undirected inquiry often leads to frustration and discomfort. The groups are encouraged to work through the anxiety, and to allow it to draw them creatively into new areas. While emotion is not in focus, it is considered useful. Frustration, chaos, and emotion can all help to create meaning if the group doesn't try to move away from them. Friction among subcultures allows participants to surface their assumptions – to see their own thoughts and those of others.

The most important practice of Bohmian dialogue is suspension. Participants try to suspend their assumptions, judgments, reactions, impulses, emotions during the process. Suspension is not the same as repressing them, postponing them, or blindly following them. It means attending to them, noticing them, and observing them without judging them as right/wrong. Your thoughts, physical sensations, and emotions are exposed so they can be seen by yourself and others. The group becomes your mirror, reflecting the content of thought and the underlying structures. The listeners mirror the assumptions they find behind what is being said. As the thought process gets observed, it changes.

A facilitator is useful in the beginning of a Bohmian dialogue to hold the group through this process. The facilitator would usually start by talking about dialogue and explaining the meaning of the word, and the principles and practices of this particular approach. S/he is not seen as a neutral outsider, but rather as a participant in the group. S/he should ideally work him/herself out of a job as soon as possible, once the group has established a dialogue practice. Bohmian dialogue is clearly very different from how we normally function. We generally pay attention to the content of our thoughts – our ideas, opinions, questions, insights - but not the process of forming them. We usually find it very difficult to let go of our judgments and ideas because we identify deeply with them, we hold on to and defend them. If we view thought as a larger system that moves through us and around us, we may be able to take a step back and to see a) how what is going on within each of us is a reflection of the dialogue group and b) how what is going on in the dialogue group is a reflection of the larger society.

Resources

Bohm, David (1996). On Dialogue

Bohm, David, **Donald Factor**, and **Peter Garrett** (1991) "Dialogue: A Proposal"

www.laetusinpraesens.org

Citizen Councils

Citizen Councils are experiments in democracy. Their purpose is to define what the people of a community, city, or nation as a whole would really want if they were to carefully think about it and talk it over with each other in dialogue.

There is a variety of different related forms, which we are roughly grouping under the header "citizen councils". These include "citizen consensus councils", "citizen deliberation councils", "wisdom councils", "citizen juries", "consensus conferences", "citizen assemblies", and "planning cells". They differ in the number of participants, selection process, mandate, meeting time and frequency, whether they are permanent or temporary, their level of expertise, media participation, etc.

The common thread of the Citizen Council is the act of collecting a small group of citizens (usually 12-24) comprising a "microcosm" of their community or society. These are not elected representatives in the political sense. They speak for themselves as individual citizens, but they embody the diverse perspectives and capacities of their wider group. Because of this composition, their decisions are likely to be similar to the decisions the wider group would have come up with if able to engage in a similar dialogue at a large scale. If their process is made visible to that wider group as it unfolds, stimulating conversations of similar quality are likely to happen informally across an extended area.

The members of the Citizen Council come together face-to-face to engage in a facilitated dialogue or deliberation around one or more issues concerning the population from which it was selected. The dialogue approach needs to be one that enables diverse members to really hear each other, to open their minds and expand their understanding, and to engage each other in seeking creative solutions. The dialogue can last a few days or longer periods of time. It usually results in a final statement released to the larger population and to the authorities. In order to come up with such an agreement, the members have to explore their diversity, go deeper to the point of common ground, and help each other to see the whole picture.

Resources

Atlee, Tom (2002). The Tao of Democracy

http://co-intelligence.org

http://www.wisedemocracy.org

Communities of Practice

Though not always explicitly named, Communities of Practice are part of everyday life. A Community of Practice is an organizational form that assists with knowledge sharing, learning and change. It is generally a self-organizing group of people who have come together to share knowledge on a particular field of practice.

The process of identifying and cultivating Communities of Practice is becoming increasingly widespread in both corporate, government, and civil society settings worldwide. This development is a response to increasing complexity and the shift to a knowledge society. The assumption here is that knowledge can no longer be packaged, externalized, and put in databases and remain relevant over time. We need to be able to draw on living, tacit, contextual knowledge, which primarily exists within people and can only be volunteered, not conscripted. Communities of Practice are designed to transmit knowledge voluntarily on a "pull" basis (as and when needed for a specific problem or situation) rather than on a "push" basis (where the expert decides what others need to know and presents it to them in a one-way communication).

This process requires strong and trustful relationships, because it relies on "know-who" in order to transmit "know-how". Communities of Practice employ a number of different dialogue tools in order to build these relationships and enable learning among their members.

The paradox of this organizational form is that it often fails if it is over-managed, but does need to be cultivated to be sustained. It requires being supported, yet left to create its own boundaries and identity to be successful. After all, relationships are largely determined by chemistry and by building trust over time.

Resources

Wenger, Etienne (1998). Communities of Practice: Learning, Meaning, and Identity

www.etiennewenger.com

Deep Ecology

Deep Ecology is both a philosophy and a movement. The term was coined by Norwegian philosopher Arne Naess to contrast with the kind of environmentalism that is motivated by purely human interests. The Deep Ecology philosophy is premised on the assumption that nonhuman life on Earth has intrinsic worth beyond its usefulness for human purposes, and that the current level of human interference with the nonhuman world is excessive. This philosophy has inspired an array of experiential and dialogic practices, primarily developed by John Seed and Joanna Macy, intended to help "decondition" people from centuries of putting human interests above all others. Macy calls this work "the Work that Reconnects".

The Work that Reconnects aims to help people experience their innate connections with each other and the web of life, so that they may become motivated to play their part in creating a sustainable civilization. Participants experience and share their innermost responses to the present condition of our world, reframe their pain for the world as evidence of their interconnectedness, and build relationships of mutual support and collaboration. They also gain concepts, exercises, and methods which help to make visible the power they have to take part in the healing of the world.

This work came mainly out of the 1970's in North America where it brought together thousands of people - antinuclear and environmental activists, psychologists, artists, and spiritual practitioners. One of the most famous exercises is called "The Council of All Beings". Here, participants take on the role of different living beings and engage from the perspective of that being in a dialogue on what is happening to their world.

Deep Ecology is really a different worldview. We include it here because it challenges and widens our conception of what dialogue can be, to include dialogue with the non-human world, as well as dialogue with our past and future. We also find that the structured exercises it offers can shift participants out of their comfort zones and into a state of openness, in which further dialogue can then take place. Macy and Brown's "Coming Back to Life: Practices to Reconnect our Lives, Our World," provides an up-to-date description of the theory behind the Work that Reconnects, some sixty exercises, both new and old, and guides to designing and facilitating workshops.

Resources

Macy, Joanna and Molly Young Brown (1998).
Coming Back to Life: Practices to Reconnect our Lives, our World

www.deepecology.org
www.joannamacy.net

Dynamic Facilitation and Choice-Creating

The most exciting and uplifting experience a group trying to solve a problem can have is to encounter a new option that has never been considered before. This option may be something that creates synergy where before there were competing proposals or something that overrides or somehow makes previous concerns irrelevant. This is what Dynamic Facilitation tries to make happen by creating a space called "Choice-Creation".

Choice-Creation brings together the openness and transformative approach of dialogue with the deliberative approach of trying to actually reach specific conclusions to specific problems. The facilitator plays an active role, helping participants to determine an issue they really care about, and to say openly, clearly, and respectfully what is on their minds about it. Throughout this process the facilitator is working with four flipcharts at the same time – lists of Solutions, Problems, Data and Concerns. As group conclusions emerge, a Decisions flipchart is added. The facilitator is constantly following the natural dynamic flow and spontaneity of the conversation, rather than trying to manage an agenda.

Dynamic facilitation was developed by Jim Rough in the early 1980's. According to Rough, it is particularly valuable in situations where people face important, complex, strategic, or seemingly impossible-to-solve issues, when there is a conflict, or when people seek to build teamwork or community.

Resources
www.ToBE.net
www.SocietysBreakthrough.com

Focus Groups

Focus groups are primarily used in the field of qualitative academic and market research. They usually consist of a relatively small group of 6-12 people. Focus Groups are brought together in the exploratory phases of a study or project in order to use the results from the conversation to help develop questionnaires or survey tools in quantitative research. The benefit of a focus group as opposed to a survey is that participants have a chance to interact, brainstorm and react to each other's comments. This helps to get more considered answers from participants, it creates possibilities for new ideas to be generated, and it also provides information about the relationships and dynamics of the group. Most importantly, a focus group helps to answer "why…" questions whereas surveys can primarily answer "what…" questions.

The focus group is particularly useful when an organization wants to start up a new project, and is unclear how the community will respond (See question box). This is generally more of a consultative process than a meeting of stakeholders who will actually be involved in acting together to implement the project. Focus Groups are not necessarily dialogic, but they can be. Other tools, such as Circle and World Café, can be used creatively within a focus group session.

Community-related questions for Focus Groups

- What are the implications for the community?

- What will their key concerns be?

- What are the obstacles that might get in the way of the success of this project?

- What are the forces that might help it succeed?

- What are the reasons behind people's preferences?

Graphic Facilitation

A picture is worth 1000 words. A graphic facilitator is skilled at visualizing what people are saying during a dialogue. When a graphic facilitator is present, a wall will be covered with white paper at the beginning of a dialogue process. At the end of the workshop that paper will colorfully tell the whole story of the process, with words, mindmaps, symbols and images. Rich pictures can capture the complexity of the discussions and the meeting in simple overview.

An information designer will listen to what people are saying throughout a process and turn it into diagrams, tables, and models. S/he will continually be reflecting back to participants their own knowledge in a different form for them to react to.

Graphic facilitation itself is not necessarily a dialogue process, but it is a an important tool that can play a major role in the quality and success of a dialogic process. It helps to make the group more aware of itself and of the patterns that are emerging in the conversation.

Learning Journeys

Learning journeys are about getting away from behind the desk, out of the comfort zone, the conference rooms and hotels. They are physical journeys from one place to another, intended to explore and experience the world first-

'The desk is a dangerous place from which to view the world.'

John le Carré

hand. These are journeys of the mind, challenging the participants' preconceived notions and assumptions about current reality and possibilities. As mentioned for most of the additional tools, they are only dialogue methods in a very broad sense – engaging in a dialogue with reality. However, the key distinction between a real learning journey and a typical "field trip" or "study tour" is created by introducing dialogue methods.

Learning journeys have to be carefully planned. Choosing an organization, community or group, clarifying your own intentions and questions, training how best to "suspend judgment" – all of these steps are part of the learning. In a learning journey the learning group is invited to sit down in small groups in empathic dialogue with local stakeholders to understand their reality. They listen not only with an open mind, but also with an open heart and open will. After a visit they hear each other's perspectives, and through conversation come to a deeper understanding and a more complete picture of what they have experienced together. They become aware of what others saw that they themselves may have been blind to, and discover the value of broadening their understanding of what it means to see. In a successful learning journey, deep learning goes beyond the learning group; it encompasses both the visitors and the visited.

Listening Projects and Dialogue Interviewing

Many of us are not used to being genuinely listened to. The most common form of listening is the kind where we are constantly judging what the speaker is saying, or waiting for an opportunity to say what we ourselves want to say. When you create an opportunity for really just asking questions, listening with an open mind, and connecting to what another person is saying, you can actually help that person to uncover a knowledge they didn't even know they had. Through an open-ended conversation delving deeply into the interviewee's life experience, knowledge, needs and concerns, the issues are brought to life in their mind and heart. They themselves realize things they hadn't seen before, about how they feel and what they can do about it.

This kind of interviewing and listening can be relevant in many situations. It may be a way to mobilize people to participate in a particular project, to develop a network, or simply to awaken them to act as individuals. As an example, "Listening Projects" are a specific form of community organizing, used since the early 1980s, in which trained interviewers go door-to-door asking citizens powerful questions about local issues. The interviews will usually last about one hour. Once the interviewees become convinced that the intentions of the interviewer are genuine, and that this person is sincerely there to listen to them and not to judge them, they will open up and share their perspectives. The project generates change not by telling people what to do, but really just by asking questions and listening.

Resources
www.listeningproject.info
www.dialogonleadership.org

Socratic Dialogue

A Socratic Dialogue is a search for truth. This approach of course draws its origins and name from the life of Socrates, the ancient Greek philosopher. It usually takes place in quite a small group, for example 6 people. The most important rule in a Socratic Dialogue is to "think for yourself". The dialogue usually starts with a philosophical question, that is, a fundamental question that can be answered by reflecting on it. Participants are invited to postpone and suspend their judgments, approaching this question with an open mind. The facilitator prods, asks questions, and gently challenges the student/participant to go more deeply into their reasoning. They strive for consensus, not because it is necessarily achievable but because the desire for consensus helps to deepen the investigation and to listen deeply to all points of view. They allow their underlying assumptions to surface, unravel, and be examined.

Key to a Socratic Dialogue is that, while the question is philosophical, it is always applied to shared concrete experience, and the group remains in contact with this experience throughout. Participants bring in specific examples, against which what is being said can be tested. Insights are jointly drawn from this in-depth understanding of concrete examples - at the same time, participants gain confidence in their own thinking.

Resources

www.socraticmethod.net

Story Dialogue

As mentioned in the section on the Circle, human beings have always used stories to communicate. Before we had writing, stories were used to convey information and wisdom across generations because they are easier to remember than isolated facts or concepts. We are in a sense, "hardwired" for stories. Yet, we tend to rationalize and dissociate the concepts we are trying to convey from personal stories that illustrate them.

The "Story Dialogue" technique was developed by Ron Labonte and Joan Featherstone when working in community development and health in Canada. They saw it as a way to bridge the gulf between practice and theory, and to recognize the expertise that people have in their own lives. It uses stories to detect important themes and issues for a community, moving from personalized experience to generalized knowledge.

In Story Dialogue, individuals are invited to write and tell their stories around a generative theme – a theme that holds energy and possibility for the group. As a person shares their story, others listen intently, sometimes taking notes. The storytelling is followed by a reflection circle where each person shares how the storyteller's story is also their story, and how it is different. A structured dialogue ensues guided by the questions: "what" (what was the story), "why" (why did events in the story happen as they did), "now what" (what are our insights) and "so what" (what are we going to do about it). The group closes by creating "insight cards", writing down each insight on a colored card and grouping these into themes.

Resources

http://www.evaluationtrust.org/tools/story.html

Theatre of the Oppressed

During the 1950's in Brazil, theatre director Augusto Boal started asking questions about why theatre is a "monologue". Why did the audience have to always be passively consuming the performance? He started experimenting with interactive theatre, creating a "dialogue" between the audience and the stage. His assumption was that dialogue is the common, healthy dynamic between all humans, and that oppression is the result of the absence of dialogue and the dominance of monologue. Over the past 50 years, the "Theatre of the Oppressed" (TO) has developed into a large system of diverse games and interactive theatre techniques, being used in communities across the world. TO is primarily created as an instrument to enable the "oppressed" to concretely transform their society, by transforming monologue into dialogue. All the TO techniques pose dilemmas and challenges to participants, related to the core social problems and power structures of their particular communities and society at large. The techniques help to move out of the head, and more into the body. This enables people to meet across diversity of cultures and levels of education, and it also allows access to more unconscious dynamics. The TO workshops, now run not only by Boal but by hundreds of facilitators, are a great training ground for action not only in theatre but in life. The most well-known form of TO is called "Forum Theatre". In Forum Theatre a dilemma is

134

posed to the group in the form of a theatrical scene, which usually has a negative outcome. Participants are asked to step into the play and take on the role of one of the actors to try to change the outcome. They are invited to imagine new possibilities and solutions, and to actively try to make them happen in the moment. As a result of the group problem solving, highly interactive imagining, physical involvement, trust, fun, and vigorous interpersonal dynamics, the participants learn how they are a part of perpetuating their own problems and how they can be the source of their own liberation.

Resources

Boal, Augusto (1992). Games for Actors and Non-Actors

http://www.theatreoftheoppressed.org

The 21st Century Town Meeting

How do you engage 5000 citizens actively in one town meeting, and enable each of them to give substantive input into public decision-making? This is what happens in the 21st Century Town Meetings of AmericaSpeaks. Updating the traditional New England town meeting to address the needs of today's democracy, AmericaSpeaks restores the citizen's voice. At the gatherings, facilitated deliberations happen at tables of 10-12 participants. Technology then transforms these discussions into synthesized recommendations. Each table submits their ideas through wireless computers, and the entire group votes on final recommendations. Results are compiled into a report in real-time for participants to take home at the end of the meeting, immediately identifying priorities and recommendations. Since the organization's founding in 1995, AmericaSpeaks methodologies have engaged over 65,000 people in over 50 large-scale forums in all 50 states and the District of Columbia. Meetings have addressed local, state and national decisions on issues ranging from Social Security reform to the development of municipal budgets and regional plans.

Resources

www.americaspeaks.org

III. Epilogue: African Conversations

This book originates in Africa. The first ideas of it were developed in Africa, the original audience it was written for was African and last but not least: The history of many of the profiled tools goes back to Africa. In embarking on this book project, we were aware that it is in some ways absurd to import dialogue methods from the West into Africa, where conversation is so deeply engrained in the indigenous culture. Given that Africa is the cradle of humankind, it may well be the place where people first sat down in circle to communicate. As we moved into looking at more recent dialogue methods, we therefore wanted to also explore and recognize this tradition

We started our inquiry into African dialogue intending to clarify and better understand the meanings of terms such as "lekgotla", "imbizo", and "indaba". These words which signify traditional African gatherings have become popularized in some countries.

We feel it is relevant for us to - at least - attempt to document briefly here what we have learned to date. However, it is important to emphasize this exploration is a universe beyond the scope of this book. Firstly, it is impossible to characterize African conversation and dialogue processes sweepingly because Africa is a continent with thousands of societal groupings each with their own particularities in terms of governance, decision-making, and community life. Secondly, the meeting forms are inseparable from the wider culture in which they are used. Thirdly, if we really want to engage with these processes in their entirety, they do challenge our fundamental assumptions and preconceptions. This section is inspired by interviews with Dr. Magomme Masoga and Nomvula Dlamini, as well as our own experience and a few readings. It should be read as a general description and is not intended to be cited as factual evidence.

Living Conversations

Imagine a "typical" traditional African village. In this village, conversation is constantly alive as an ongoing process from family to communal level. Women are meeting by the river during the day, young men and boys talk while herding cows, families gather around the fire and share stories. Conversations weave together. Through oral history,

story-telling, and proverbs, the principles and rules for the community are shared and alive.

These ongoing conversations are a way of life. The men of the village do gather in specifically convened meetings (lekgotlas or imbizos) as necessary, where they come to an overview of what is going on in the village and take decisions. But this is only a small part of the village conversation. The women, youth and families converse outside and influence the conversation that takes place at the lekgotla. When conversations happen, it is always with an engrained awareness that these are not just individuals communicating. Each person is connected to a family, a community, and a group of ancestors. They represent a larger whole. They do not just speak for themselves or interact just on their own behalf.

'In the end our purpose is social and communal harmony and wellbeing. Ubuntu does not say 'I think therefore I am.' It says rather 'I am human because I belong. I participate. I share."

Archbishop Desmond Tutu

Communication is not only direct and verbal. Art, drama, drumming, and song are used as ways to communicate, especially about things that may be difficult to confront. Women in particular may compose a new song to communicate what is going on for them. The community is in some ways even architecturally designed for conversation and meeting. The houses are circular, the fireplace is circular, and the houses in relation to each other make up a circle. The conversation is embedded in the physical space.

The Lekgotla

The Lekgotla process of Botswana is likely to be the most well-documented African council process of Southern Africa. It is often criticized these days because it has to be convened by the Chief and only includes the men of the village, but many argue that there are other ways for the women and youth to get their issues across to the Lekgotla. (In the Venda culture of Northern South Africa, apparently the final decisions must still pass by the matriarch of the village.) We feel it is useful to draw lessons from this process even for dialogues across genders, though it may be inappropriate to label such dialogues "Lekgotla".

In the village, the decision to convene the Lekgotla is not necessarily transparent. The chief's counselors play a role of listening in the community and paying attention to issues as they arise. When something is building up they bring it to the Lekgotla to make sure that conversation happens as early as possible before a conflict escalates.

A Lekgotla is always held in the open air because the outdoors belongs to no one. This provides a sense of freedom, openness and invitation to people to attend and speak honestly. There is also no time limit on the process. It may go on for days or even weeks until the issues being addressed have reached resolution. According to Nomvula Dlamini, *"People's lives unfolded into time. Time wasn't imposed on people's lives."* This is a whole different conception of time from that of the modern world, and it is a fundamental frame of mind. Nomvula points out that this freedom from time restrictions enables participants to suspend judgment and be willing to listen to someone's point of view and story *in context* without rushing them.

The Lekgotla meets in a circle. The circle represents unity, and the participants are aware that it is only if they are whole and united that they can address their problems. The circle also ensures that they face each other and speak honestly to one another. As they gather, they greet each person around the circle. They make sure that those who really matter to the process are present. Though they may be seated by rank and speak in order of a hierarchy, the emphasis is on every voice being heard equally.

The conversation is opened up. Each person in turn talks about how the issue affects their lives directly. Nothing is seen as an isolated event. All the stories are heard in context, respectfully, and taking the time it needs to take. The different orientation to time allows for a deeper quality of listening, and every voice is listened to and given equal weight. The same person won't speak twice or respond until they've heard the views of others. Silence is also an integral part of the conversation as in between each voice the words are allowed to sink in. Emotion is expressed freely but constructively. The process enables each participant to reflect on and assess his own behavior in relation to the community.

The Lekgotla is partly a court, passing judgment on conflicts, but it can also be a more general gathering for conversations around the main issues facing the village. When resolving injustices, the focus is less on determining right and wrong or on punishment, and more on healing, restoration of relationships, and finding ways of moving on. The accused is always heard first in the process of clarifying what happened, but he is also given a chance to assess at the end whether he thinks the group's decision is fair and whether the rehabilitation and restoration he is being requested to undertake is within his means. He is never silenced.

The group takes collective responsibility for the issues. The solutions are explored meaningfully together, rather than imposed from one side, and the orientation is towards consensus and compromise. The community's collective need is at the center, above any individual's needs, and the concern is always what is best for the community. To the Western mind, this may sound oppressive, but in this culture it is not seen as sacrifice because what is good for the collective is completely intertwined with what is good for the individual. The concept of freedom is that you should have the maximum degree of freedom as long as it is not at the expense of the freedom of others.

Through the community's ongoing conversation there is a level of shared clarity around the principles and sense of right and wrong. These principles are then applied through the deliberation at the Lekgotla to determine what should be done in the particular context. There is no law outlining a standardized regulation for each situation.

Drawing Lessons

Some of the deeply held worldviews behind the integral nature of conversation in a traditional African community may seem incompatible with modern life. The idea that we are not first and foremost individuals but members of a community, and that we do not need to be slaves to the clock are difficult to practice in their entirety. But exploring

African culture can challenge our mindsets and it's certainly possible to draw inspiration and to see how the nature of our conversations changes if we try to shift our worldview.

Many of the tools and processes in this collection have taken part of their inspiration from similar underlying views and cultural practices as those we know from the traditional African village described above. Some have found their inspiration directly from the soil of Africa, others from Native American traditions that share similar beliefs. Many of them share a return to circular time, to the people and the purpose for coming together being more important than timing and structure. Most of them make use of the circle as a way of coming together in an unbroken whole.

Dialogue is in many ways about creating a culture of coming together as a whole – letting each voice be heard, but in service to the community and the whole. Many of the methods that we are presenting seem to be coming back to much of what we already know from our own culture and history in Africa. And so while at first it may look inappropriate to be bringing in western methods to a place from which dialogue and conversation may have originated, there is something affirming in the way many of these methods are coming back to some of our very own roots. Many of the processes also recognize and work explicitly with story telling as a way of sharing inspired knowledge and building on memories of the best of what is and was.

About the Authors

Marianne Mille Bojer [bojer@reospartners.com]

Mille is an experienced facilitator and designer of group dialogue and change processes. She has recently relocated to Sao Paulo to set up Reos Brasil. Reos is an international group of firms focused on leadership development and social innovation in complex systems. Mille was previously based in South Africa with Reos Social Innovation, where her work was focused on leadership development and multistakeholder projects addressing the challenges of HIV/AIDS and orphaned and vulnerable children. Mille is also one of the founders of Pioneers of Change (www.pioneersofchange.net), a learning community of young change agents across the world. During the course of her work with Pioneers of Change she developed extensive experience in facilitating learning communities, hosting dialogue, as well as in network- and organization-building. Her academic background is in international development studies. Born in Denmark, she has spent more than half her life abroad in Egypt, the United States, Burkina Faso, The Netherlands, Brazil, and South Africa.

Heiko Roehl [hr@heikoroehl.de]

As a designer of social development interventions, Heiko is passionate about generating alternative futures. He is Head of Corporate Organization at the German Technical Cooperation (GTZ), an international enterprise for sustainable development with operations in more than 120 countries implementing developmental programmes on behalf of the German Government. From 2002 to 2006, he was seconded to the Nelson Mandela Foundation in Johannesburg/ South Africa by the

German Federal Ministry of Economic Cooperation and Development to support the organizational development of Nelson Mandela's legacy organization in the fight against HIV/AIDS. Prior to that, he spent more than six years at Daimler's *Society and Technology Research* Think Tank in Berlin and Paolo Alto working on the future of organizational value creation, strategic foresight, knowledge organizations and tools of change management. His academic background is in psychology and organizational theory, he holds a PhD in sociology and has published widely on organizational and societal change (see: www.heikoroehl.de for further Infomation). Passionate about linking the practictioner's experiences to the theories of organizational change and development, Heiko is Editor of the German Journal of Organizational Development and Change Management (www.zoe.ch).

Marianne Knuth [knuth@reospartners.com]

 Marianne is a facilitator of individual and group learning and co-creation. She has recently moved to South Africa from Zimbabwe as a Partner of Reos Social Innovation. In South Africa Marianne's work is primarily focusing on multistakeholder dialogue and action around the challenge of orphans and vulnerable children at national level as well as being part of a local community initiative to develop innovative solutions to build the community's capacity to serve the children. In Zimbabwe, she founded Kufunda Learning Village, a learning centre aimed at the creation of locally rooted solutions to community self-reliance challenges, through the use of people's own imagination, collaboration and resources. Through this work Marianne was elected an Ashoka Fellow (www.ashoka.org) in 2004. Since 2001 she has also been teaching courses on the art of hosting meaningful and strategic conversations. In 1999 she co-founded Pioneers of Change with Mille and Colleen. She holds a masters degree in international business and finance from the business school of Copenhagen. During her studies she served as president AIESEC International (www.aiesec.net), a global student organisation of primarily business students, spanning 87 countries and roughly 50,000 students.

Colleen Magner [magner@reospartners.com]

Colleen's expertise areas are social entrepreneurship and out-of-classroom learning methods, focusing on dialogue and experiential learning. She is a Partner of Reos Social Innovation, based in Johannesburg. She is also a faculty member at the Gordon Institute of Business Science (GIBS), and previously managed the Policy, Leadership and Gender Studies Unit (PL&G) at GIBS. She has supervised a number of teaching cases on social entrepreneurship, and edited the book: "Dust to Diamonds: Stories of South African Social Entrepreneurs."

Previous to GIBS, Colleen co-founded Pioneers of Change with Mille and Marianne. Colleen graduated from the University of Port Elizabeth, South Africa, with a dual degree in Law and Economics, and has a Masters degree in Organisational Change and Knowledge Management from the University of Kwa Zulu Natal. She has also attended the following executive programmes: "Making Markets Work" and "Teaching the Practice of Management", both offered by Harvard Business School.

Appendix A
Overview on Purpose Assessment

Purpose of the Dialogue Process										
Generating Awareness	Problem-solving	Building Relationships	Sharing Knowledge	Innovation	Shared Vision	Capacity Building	Pers./Leaders. Development	Dealing with Conflict	Strategy/Action Planning	Decision Making
Appreciative Inquiry										
✓✓	✓	✓✓	✓✓	✓✓	✓✓✓	✓	✓✓	✓	✓✓✓	✓✓
Change Lab										
✓✓✓	✓✓	✓✓	✓✓	✓✓✓	✓✓	✓✓	✓✓	✓	✓✓✓	✓✓
The Circle										
✓✓	✓✓	✓✓✓	✓✓	✓✓	✓✓✓	✓	✓✓	✓✓	✓	✓✓
Deep Democracy										
✓✓✓	✓✓	✓✓	✓	✓✓	✓	✓✓	✓✓	✓✓✓	✓	✓✓✓
Future Search										
✓✓	✓✓	✓✓	✓✓	✓✓	✓✓✓	✓	✓	✓	✓✓✓	✓✓
The Israeli-Palestinian School for Peace										
✓✓	✓✓	✓✓✓	✓✓✓	✓	✓✓	✓✓	✓✓	✓✓✓	✓	✓
Open Space Technology										
✓✓	✓✓✓	✓✓	✓✓	✓✓	✓✓	✓✓	✓✓	✓✓	✓✓✓	✓✓
Scenario Planning										
✓✓	✓✓	✓✓	✓✓	✓✓✓	✓✓✓	✓	✓✓	✓	✓✓✓	✓✓
Sustained Dialogue										
✓✓✓	✓✓	✓✓✓	✓✓✓	✓	✓✓	✓	✓✓	✓✓	✓✓	✓
The World Café										
✓✓	✓✓✓	✓✓✓	✓✓✓	✓✓	✓✓	✓✓	✓✓	✓	✓	✓

Appendix B:
Overview on Context Assessment

Context of the Dialogue Process										
Situation				Participants						Facilitation
Low Complexity	High Complexity	Conflictual Situation	Peaceful Situation	Small Group (up to 30)	Large Group	Microcosm/multi-Stakeholder	Peergroup	Diversity of Power Levels	Diversity Of Culture	Specific Training Requirements
Appreciative Inquiry										
✓✓✓	✓✓	✓	✓✓✓	✓✓✓	✓✓✓	✓	✓✓✓	✓	✓✓	✓
Change Lab										
✓	✓✓✓	✓✓	✓✓	✓✓✓	✓	✓✓✓	✓	✓✓	✓✓	✓✓
The Circle										
✓✓	✓✓	✓✓	✓✓✓	✓✓✓	✓	✓✓	✓✓✓	✓✓	✓✓✓	✓
Deep Democracy										
✓✓	✓✓	✓✓✓	✓✓	✓✓✓	✓	✓✓✓	✓✓	✓✓	✓✓	✓✓✓
Future Search										
✓✓	✓✓✓	✓✓	✓✓	✓	✓✓	✓✓✓	✓	✓✓	✓✓	✓✓
The Israeli-Palestinian School for Peace										
✓	✓✓	✓✓✓	✓	✓✓✓	✓	✓✓	✓✓	✓✓✓	✓✓	✓✓✓
Open Space Technology										
✓✓✓	✓✓✓	✓✓✓	✓✓✓	✓✓✓	✓✓✓	✓✓✓	✓✓✓	✓✓✓	✓✓✓	✓✓✓
Scenario Planning										
✓	✓✓✓	✓	✓✓	✓✓	✓✓	✓✓✓	✓	✓✓	✓✓	✓✓
Sustained Dialogue										
✓	✓✓	✓✓	✓	✓✓✓	✓	✓✓	✓✓	✓✓	✓✓	✓✓
The World Café										
✓✓	✓✓	✓✓	✓✓	✓✓	✓✓✓	✓✓	✓✓	✓✓✓	✓✓✓	✓